ideals

Soup, Salad, Sandwich COOKBOOK

by June Turner and Naomi Arbit

Ideals Publishing Corp.
Milwaukee, Wisconsin

Introduction

Never again will you think of soups, salads and sandwiches as ho-hum, humdrum and ordinary. Authors Arbit and Turner bring their gourmet ingenuity to their fifth cookbook, proving that the most common soups, salads, and sandwiches can be made most uncommonly delightful.

Thick and robust, hot and hearty, soup is the universal comforter against winter's chill. Ladled ceremoniously from a steaming tureen, soup can provide the spark for glowing, convivial dining. But it can also be a chilled cooler for those long, hot summer evenings. Prepare the soup early in the morning and simmer it all day to fill the house with a welcome-home aroma. Or use on-the-shelf ingredients for a punctual finale to a busy day.

To some, sandwiches evoke memories of a peanut butter and jelly intrusion into childhood's playtime. But, there are sandwiches, and then there are *sandwiches*. We present a smorgasbord of hot, cold, meat, fish, egg, cheese and vegetable sandwiches which will show you just how spectacular a sandwich can be.

Salads can be more than just a little bit of lettuce and a slice of tomato. We have included a great variety of salads which can subtly introduce a dinner, tantalizingly accompany the meal, or efficiently stand as the main course.

It will take only a small sampling of the recipes in the *Soup, Salad, Sandwich Cookbook* to show you that these mealtime staples need never be ordinary or commonplace again.

ISBN 0-8249-3001-0

Copyright © MCMLXXXI by Naomi Arbit and June Turner
All rights reserved.
Printed and bound in the United States of America

Published by Ideals Publishing Corporation
11315 Watertown Plank Road
Milwaukee, WI 53226
Published simultaneously in Canada

Contents

Soups

Super Soups

Hot soup brings a glow to wintry days, filling the house with a tantalizing aroma. Served with bread and salad, soup makes a complete meal. Any leftovers keep well when refrigerated or frozen and make the perfect lunch or supper for another day.

Soup is not just for the winter months. During the hot summer, cold soups make a refreshing beginning to a meal or just the thing for lunch. Some require cooking before chilling, but can be prepared in the cool of the evening and chilled overnight for the next day's luncheon or dinner. Adjust seasonings after chilling, for a perfect flavor.

The Stockpot

Beef Stock

    4 pounds beef shank and short ribs
    5 quarts water
    2 medium onions, chopped
    1 carrot, cut up
    1 tablespoon tomato paste
    2 sprigs parsley, chopped
    1 bay leaf
    2 whole cloves
    1 teaspoon thyme

Place beef shank and short ribs in shallow pan and bake at 400° for 2 hours, turning once. Combine beef, drippings and remaining ingredients in a large stockpot. Bring to a boil; reduce heat and simmer, uncovered, for about 4 hours. Refrigerate for 4 hours. Skim fat and strain. Makes approximately 3 quarts.

Chicken Stock I

Use this basic chicken stock whenever chicken stock is called for in soups, casseroles and sauces.

    3 chicken bouillon cubes dissolved in 1½ cups
        hot water, or 1½ teaspoons chicken bouillon
        crystals in 1¼ cups hot water, or canned
        chicken broth.
    4 pounds chicken backs, necks, wings or
        1 small stewing hen
    4 quarts water
    1 large onion, diced
    3 ribs celery, diced
    1 large carrot, sliced
    1 turnip, diced
    ½ cup minced parsley
    1 teaspoon thyme
    ½ teaspoon savory
    1 teaspoon salt

Place all ingredients in a stockpot. Simmer for 2 to 3 hours, until reduced by half. Cool, strain and season with salt and pepper. Refrigerate until needed. If desired, puree vegetables in a blender and add to stock. If stock is made with a stewing hen, remove meat from bones and store for other uses. Makes approximately 3 quarts.

Chicken Stock II

This stock with a touch of garlic is intended for soups with a heartier flavor.

    4 pounds chicken backs, necks, wings
        or 1 small stewing hen
    4 quarts water
    ½ cup tomato paste
    1 small onion, studded with 6 whole cloves
    2 ribs celery and leaves, chopped
    ½ cup chopped cabbage
    ½ teaspoon allspice
    1 garlic clove, minced
    1 bay leaf
    1 teaspoon salt
    ¼ teaspoon pepper

Place all ingredients in a stockpot. Simmer, uncovered, for 2 to 3 hours, until liquid is somewhat reduced. Cool and strain. Refrigerate until needed. If stock is made with a stewing hen, remove meat from bones and store for other uses. Makes approximately 3 quarts.

Fish Stock

    2 tablespoons margarine or butter
    1 large onion, chopped
    2 ribs celery, chopped
    1 carrot, chopped
    3 pounds non-oily fish
    7 cups water
    1 cup dry white wine
    1 teaspoon thyme
    ½ cup chopped parsley

Melt butter in a stockpot. Add onion, celery and carrot; sauté until onion is tender. Add remaining ingredients and bring to a boil. Skim foam and reduce heat. Simmer for 1 hour. Strain before using. Can be frozen. Makes approximately 3 quarts.

Minestrone

Hearty Italian vegetable soup.

¼ pound salt pork, diced
1 tablespoon olive oil
1 medium onion, chopped
1 clove garlic, minced
5 cups chicken stock
1 large can tomatoes
1 carrot, sliced
1 rib celery, chopped
¼ head cabbage, shredded
1 zucchini, sliced
1 1-pound can garbanzo beans, drained
1 1-pound can kidney beans, drained
1 teaspoon salt
½ teaspoon pepper
1 teaspoon oregano
¼ cup chopped parsley
1 cup macaroni
    Grated Parmesan cheese

In a stockpot sauté salt pork until brown. Add olive oil, onion and garlic; sauté until onion is tender. Add remaining ingredients, except macaroni and cheese. Simmer for 2 to 3 hours. Add macaroni and cook for 10 to 15 minutes, or until macaroni is tender. Garnish with Parmesan cheese. Serve with crusty bread and butter. Makes 6 to 8 servings.

Chicken Vegetable Soup

7 cups Chicken Stock (Recipe on page 4)
3 cups assorted vegetables, such as broccoli, cauliflower, tomatoes, carrots, onions, celery, turnip, cabbage, peas, green beans
½ cup dry white wine
2 cups chopped cooked chicken

Bring stock to a boil in a stockpot. Add vegetables and wine. Simmer for 20 minutes. Stir in chicken. Serve with bread and cheese. Makes 10 to 12 servings.

Caldo Verde

2 10¾-ounce cans chicken broth
1 cup water
1 10-ounce package frozen, chopped spinach
¼ pound boiled ham, cubed
¼ cup instant mashed potatoes

In a saucepan, combine chicken broth, water, spinach and ham. Bring to a boil. Reduce heat and simmer for 5 minutes, stirring to separate spinach. Stir in instant potatoes. Simmer a few minutes longer or until slightly thickened. Makes 6 servings.

Jambalaya

2 to 3 strips bacon
1 medium onion, chopped
1 clove garlic, minced
1 rib celery, chopped
1 green pepper, chopped
1 28-ounce can tomatoes
½ 6-ounce can tomato paste
3 cups chicken broth
½ teaspoon thyme
1 bay leaf
1 teaspoon sugar
1 teaspoon salt
    Dash red pepper
2 to 3 cooked pork sausages, diced
1 cup diced cooked chicken
½ pound cooked ham, cut in strips
1 pound cooked shrimp
3 cups cooked rice
¼ cup minced parsley

Fry bacon; drain and set aside. Sauté onion, garlic, celery and pepper in bacon fat for a few minutes. Add tomatoes, tomato paste, broth, thyme, bay leaf, sugar, salt and red pepper. Simmer for 25 to 30 minutes. Add meats, shrimp and rice. Add more water if necessary. Sprinkle with parsley and serve. Makes 8 servings.

Bouillabaisse

2 medium onions, sliced
1 clove garlic, minced
⅓ cup olive oil
1 28-ounce can tomatoes
1 16-ounce can tomatoes
2 pounds frozen flounder fillets, thawed and cut into fingers
1 7½-ounce can crab meat, drained and cartilage removed *or* ½-pound fresh
1 7½-ounce can chopped clams and juice
1 1-pound package frozen shrimp, thawed
1 teaspoon chicken bouillon granules
1 bay leaf
½ cup chopped pimiento
2 dashes Tabasco sauce
¼ cup dried parsley flakes
½ teaspoon thyme
½ teaspoon saffron
1 cup dry white wine

In a stockpot, sauté onion and garlic in olive oil until golden. Add tomatoes, flounder, crab meat, clams, shrimp, bouillon granules and bay leaf. Simmer 15 to 20 minutes. Add pimiento, Tabasco sauce, parsley, thyme, saffron and wine. Turn heat to low, cover, and let stand for 10 minutes. Makes 8 to 10 servings.

Hearty Soup

Winter Vegetable Soup

- 1 17-ounce can whole kernel corn with liquid
- 1 cup diced carrot
- 1 cup diced celery
- 2 tablespoons minced onion
- 2 potatoes, diced
- 1 46-ounce can tomato juice
- 2 tablespoons butter
- 3 cups water
- 2 teaspoons sugar
  Salt and pepper to taste
- 1 10-ounce package frozen peas

In a stockpot, combine all ingredients except peas. Bring to a boil. Reduce heat and simmer, uncovered, 45 minutes. Add peas and simmer an additional 3 to 5 minutes. Makes 8 to 10 servings.

Maryland Crab Soup

- 1 pound beef bones
- 2 quarts water
- 1 small onion, chopped
- 2 ribs celery, chopped
- 2 1-pound cans tomatoes
- 2 teaspoons salt
- 1 teaspoon thyme
- ½ teaspoon pepper
- ¼ teaspoon red pepper
- 5 cups fresh vegetables, such as zucchini, string beans, corn, peas, carrots, potatoes, peppers, lima beans, or 2 10-ounce packages frozen mixed or soup vegetables
- 1 pound crab meat
- ½ pound crab claw in shell

Place first 9 ingredients in a stockpot and simmer, covered, for 3 hours. Add remaining ingredients and simmer, covered, for 20 to 25 minutes. Remove bones and crab shell. Makes about 5 quarts.

Black Bean Soup

- 2 tablespoons vegetable oil
- 1 rib celery, chopped
- 1 medium onion, chopped
- 1 carrot, peeled and sliced
- 2 quarts water
- 2 cups black beans, soaked overnight and drained
- 1 ham bone *or* 2 smoked ham hocks *or* 1 smoked turkey leg or wing
- 1 bay leaf
- ½ teaspoon dry mustard
- 1 clove garlic
- 2 teaspoons salt
- ¼ cup sherry
  Lemon slices for garnish

In a small frypan, heat oil; sauté celery, onion and carrot until tender. Set aside. In a stockpot, combine water, beans, and ham bone. Add sautéed vegetables and drippings, bay leaf, dry mustard, garlic and salt. Simmer, covered, 3 to 4 hours or until beans are soft. Remove bone, bay leaf and garlic. Pour soup into blender or food processor and blend until smooth. Return to stockpot and heat to steaming. Just before serving, add sherry. Serve garnished with thin lemon slices. Makes 8 to 10 servings.

Oyster Soup

- 3 tablespoons butter
- 1 small onion, minced
- 1 pint oysters, drained, reserve liquid
- 1 quart milk
- 1 teaspoon salt
- ½ teaspoon pepper
- ½ teaspoon celery salt
  Minced parsley

Melt butter in a 2-quart saucepan. Sauté onion until golden. Add oysters and stir until their edges curl. Add milk, oyster liquid and seasonings and heat to steaming. Do *not* boil. Serve immediately. Garnish with minced parsley. Makes 4 to 6 servings.

Cioppino

From Fisherman's Wharf in San Francisco.

- 2 1-pound cans plum tomatoes
- 1 small onion, chopped
- 1 green pepper, chopped
- 2 tablespoons chopped parsley
- 1 8-ounce can tomato sauce
- 2 cloves garlic, minced
- 2 teaspoons salt
- ¼ teaspoon pepper
- ½ teaspoon crushed oregano
- ¼ teaspoon crushed basil
- 1 10 to 12-ounce can whole clams, drained, reserve liquid
- 1 pound flounder or cod, cut into large pieces
- 1 pound red snapper, cut into large pieces
- ½ pound shrimp, shelled and deveined

In a stockpot, combine tomatoes, onion, green pepper, parsley, tomato sauce, garlic, salt, pepper, oregano, basil and clam liquid; bring to a boil. Reduce heat, cover and simmer for 30 minutes. Add clams and fish; return to boiling. Reduce heat, cover and simmer for 30 minutes. Add shrimp the last 10 minutes of cooking time. Makes 8 servings.

Hearty Soup

Turkey Chowder

    2 cups cubed potatoes
    1 10-ounce package frozen baby lima beans
    ½ cup chopped onion
    ½ cup sliced celery
    ¼ teaspoon salt
    ⅛ teaspoon pepper
    2 cups water
    1 16-ounce can tomatoes, cut up, reserve juice
    1 10½-ounce can cream of chicken soup
    1½ cups chopped cooked turkey
    ½ cups shredded Cheddar cheese (optional)

Combine potatoes, lima beans, onion, celery, salt and pepper in a 3-quart saucepan. Blend water with tomatoes and juice. Add to vegetables. Cook, covered, for 35 to 40 minutes or until vegetables are tender. Add cream of chicken soup and turkey; simmer for 15 minutes. If desired, sprinkle each bowl of chowder with 1 tablespoon shredded cheese. Makes 8 servings.

Chicken Curry Soup

    2 tablespoons butter
    ½ tablespoon curry powder
    2 tablespoons flour
    7 cups chicken broth
    1 cup cooked chicken, cut in thin slivers
    ½ cup light cream
    ½ cup toasted, slivered almonds
    ½ cup chopped chives

Melt butter in a Dutch oven. Add curry powder and sauté for 3 minutes. Add flour and stir until blended. Slowly stir in chicken broth. Cook for 10 minutes. Just before serving, add chicken and cream; heat through. Garnish with almonds and chives. This soup may be served chilled. Makes 8 to 10 cups.

Lentil Soup

    2 cups lentils, soaked overnight and drained
    2 quarts chicken or turkey stock
    1 ham bone or smoked turkey leg or wing (optional)
    1 small onion, minced
    1 turnip, minced
    1 rib celery, minced
    1 clove garlic, minced or crushed
    1 tablespoon tomato paste
    1 pound pork sausage, cooked, crumbled
      and drained

In a Dutch oven, combine all ingredients except sausage. Bring to a boil; reduce heat and simmer for 2 hours. Add sausage and simmer an additional 1 hour. Makes 8 to 10 servings.

Cabbage and Kraut Borscht
Stock

    2 pounds beef chuck roast, cubed
    2 pounds meaty soup bones
    3 quarts water
    1 carrot, cut into chunks
    ½ onion, quartered
    1 rib celery, cut in large pieces
    1 teaspoon thyme
    ½ teaspoon pepper
    1 bay leaf

Combine all ingredients in a stockpot. Bring to a boil; reduce heat and skim. Simmer, uncovered, for 2 hours, or until the beef is tender. Remove beef and bones; skim fat from stock. Remove meat from bones; cut up and set aside.

    2 pounds cabbage, coarsely shredded
    1 16-ounce can sauerkraut, drained
    1 rib celery, sliced
    2 carrots, sliced
    1 medium onion, sliced
    1 16-ounce can tomatoes, cut up
    4 teaspoons instant beef bouillon
    ¼ cup granulated sugar
    ½ cup lemon juice
    2 teaspoons salt

Prepare Stock. Add all ingredients to Stock and simmer for 1 hour, or until cabbage is tender. Return beef to soup. Heat through and serve. Makes approximately 4 quarts.

Meatball Soup

    1 slice bread
    ½ cup milk
    1 pound ground chuck
    ½ teaspoon salt
    ½ teaspoon pepper
    2 tablespoons vegetable oil
    3 cups beef stock
    2 8-ounce cans tomato sauce with tomato bits
    1 medium onion, minced
    1 turnip, diced
    1 20-ounce package frozen soup vegetables
    1 teaspoon salt
    ¼ teaspoon allspice
    ¼ teaspoon garlic powder

Place bread and milk in a large bowl. Soak bread. Add meat, salt and pepper; mix well. Form into 24 small meatballs. Brown meatballs in oil; drain. Add remaining ingredients and simmer, uncovered, for 1 hour. Makes 4 to 6 servings.

Vegetable Soup

- 2 tablespoons margarine or vegetable oil, if needed
- 1 1-pound chuck roast, cut into 1-inch cubes
- 1 soup bone
- 2 19-ounce cans tomatoes, chopped
- 4 cups water
- 1 turnip, peeled and diced
- ¼ head cabbage, shredded
- 1 carrot, peeled and diced
- 1 zucchini, sliced
- 1 medium onion, diced
- 2 teaspoons salt
- 2 teaspoons thyme
- ½ cup Burgundy
- 1 large package frozen soup vegetables

Melt margarine in a Dutch oven; brown meat. Stir in remaining ingredients and simmer 2 to 3 hours. Remove soup bone. Tastes even better on the second day. Makes 4 to 6 servings.

New England Clam Chowder

- ¼ pound bacon, cooked and crumbled, reserve 2 tablespoons drippings
- 1 cup chopped onion
- 3 10½-ounce cans minced clams, drained, reserve broth
  Water
- 3 cups diced potatoes
- 1 teaspoon salt
- ¼ teaspoon white pepper
- 2 cups milk
- ¼ cup butter or margarine
  Chopped parsley

Heat bacon drippings in a Dutch oven. Add onion and sauté until tender. Combine reserved broth with water to make 2 cups. Add broth, potatoes, salt and pepper. Bring to a boil. Reduce heat, cover and simmer for 20 minutes, or until potatoes are tender. Add clams, milk and butter. Reheat, but do *not* boil. Garnish with bacon and parsley. Makes approximately 2 quarts.

Seafood Gumbo

- ½ cup margarine
- 4 tablespoons flour
- 1 quart water
- 2 8-ounce cans tomato sauce
- 1 10-ounce package frozen okra
- 1 teaspoon salt
- ½ teaspoon sugar
- 1 pound cod or snapper fillets
- 1 pound shrimp, peeled and deveined
- ½ pound crab meat
- 1 teaspoon basil

Melt margarine in a stockpot. Add flour and blend to make a smooth paste. Add water, tomato sauce, okra and salt. Simmer, covered, for 1 hour. Add remaining ingredients 15 minutes prior to serving. Simmer for 15 minutes. May be served over cooked rice. Makes 8 to 10 servings.

Manhattan-Style Clam Chowder

- 2 7- to 8-ounce cans minced clams, drained, reserve broth
- 1 bottle clam broth
- ¼ cup butter
- 1 cup diced onion
- 2 potatoes, diced
- 1 cup diced celery
- ¾ cup diced carrots
- ¼ cup diced green pepper
- 1 35-ounce can Italian-style plum tomatoes
- 1½ teaspoons crushed thyme
- ¼ teaspoon pepper
- ⅛ teaspoon oregano

Combine bottled clam broth with reserved broth to make 2 cups. Melt butter in a large saucepan. Add onions and sauté until golden. Add all ingredients, except clams. Add water, if necessary, to cover vegetables. Bring to a boil. Reduce heat, cover and simmer for 30 minutes, or until vegetables are tender. Add clams, remove from heat and let stand for 2 minutes or until clams are heated through. Makes 6 servings.

Split Pea Soup

- 2 cups split peas, soaked overnight and drained
- 2 quarts water or chicken stock
- 1 ham bone *or* 2 smoked ham hocks *or* 1 smoked turkey leg or wing
- 1 medium onion, chopped
- 1 carrot, peeled and sliced
- 1 rib celery, chopped
- 1 small white potato, peeled and sliced
- ½ teaspoon thyme
- 1 bay leaf
- ¼ cup minced parsley
- 1 teaspoon salt
- ¼ cup sherry
  Sour cream

In a Dutch oven, combine all ingredients except sherry and sour cream. Bring to a boil; reduce heat and simmer for 3 to 4 hours or until peas are soft. Remove bone and bay leaf. Pour soup into food processor or blender; blend until smooth. Return to Dutch oven and heat to steaming. Add sherry and serve garnished with a dollop of sour cream. Makes 8 to 10 servings.

Spinach Soup

Creamy, delicate, and smooth, with just a hint of nutmeg.

    2 cups chicken stock
    1 pound fresh spinach
    2 tablespoons butter
    ½ small onion, minced
    2 tablespoons flour
    2 cups milk
    ½ teaspoon salt
    ⅛ teaspoon nutmeg
    1 hard-boiled egg, chopped

In a saucepan, bring chicken stock to a boil. Add spinach and cook, covered, until tender. Pour into blender and blend until smooth. In a stockpot melt butter; add onion and sauté until tender. Blend in flour until smooth. Stir in milk; cook until thickened. Add blended spinach and stock; heat until steaming. Add salt and nutmeg. Serve, garnished with chopped egg. Makes 5 to 6 cups.

French Onion Soup I

    3 tablespoons butter
    6 onions, thinly sliced
    6 cups beef stock (Recipe on page 2) *or*
      4 10-ounce cans consommé
    ½ cup Burgundy
    1 cup grated Parmesan cheese
    1 cup toasted croutons (optional)

In a stockpot, melt butter; sauté onion until golden. Add broth and wine and simmer for 15 minutes. Serve sprinkled with cheese and croutons. Makes 4 to 6 servings.

French Onion Soup II

    ¼ cup butter or margarine
    6 medium onions, thinly sliced
    6 cups beef stock (Recipe on page 4) *or*
      4 10-ounce cans beef consommé
    ¼ cup sherry
    6 slices French bread, toasted
    ½ cup grated Gruyere cheese

In a stockpot, melt butter; sauté onion until tender. Add stock and simmer 20 minutes. Stir in sherry. Pour soup into individual ovenproof soup crocks or soup tureen. Float toast on top and sprinkle with cheese. Broil 4 inches from heat, until cheese melts and begins to brown. Serve at once. Makes 6 servings.

Sherry Beef Consommé

    2 10½-ounce cans beef consommé
    1 cup water
    ⅓ cup dry sherry
    6 thin slices lemon

Place consommé and water in a saucepan. Bring to a boil; reduce heat. Stir in sherry. Serve garnished with a slice of lemon. Makes 6 servings.

Curried Pea Soup

    2 cups chicken broth
    1 10-ounce package frozen green peas, thawed
    1 small onion, chopped
    1 clove garlic
    2 teaspoons curry powder
    ½ teaspoon dry mustard

Set aside 1 cup chicken broth. Combine remaining ingredients in blender or processor and whirl until smooth. In stockpot, combine puree and reserved chicken broth and heat to steaming. Makes 4 servings.

Avocado Bisque

    2 tablespoons butter
    ¼ cup minced onion
    2 tablespoons flour
    3 cups chicken broth
    1 tablespoon lemon juice
    1 tablespoon tarragon vinegar plus ¼ teaspoon
      crushed tarragon
    1 tablespoon horseradish
    1 teaspoon salt
    ¼ teaspoon pepper
    ¼ teaspoon curry powder
    1 large, ripe avocado, peeled, pit removed
    1 cup milk
    1 cup light cream

Melt butter in a heavy saucepan. Add onion and sauté until tender, but not golden. Blend in flour. Stir in chicken broth and heat, stirring constantly, until mixture comes to a boil and thickens. Add lemon juice, vinegar, horseradish and seasonings. Cover and simmer for 10 minutes. Cut avocado into chunks and place in a blender with 1 cup of the broth mixture; blend until smooth. Pour puree into soup; mix well. Stir in milk and cream and bring just to a boil. Cover and simmer 5 minutes. Makes 8 servings.

Meatless Soup

Cauliflower-Cheese Soup

- 1 cup chicken stock
- 1 small head cauliflower, broken into flowerets
- ¼ cup butter or margarine
- ½ small onion, minced
- ¼ cup flour
- 3 cups milk
- 1 cup grated Cheddar cheese
- ¼ cup grated Romano cheese
- ¼ cup minced parsley

In a medium-size saucepan, bring chicken stock to a boil. Add cauliflower and cook about 8 minutes, or until tender-crisp. Remove about one-third of the cauliflower and set aside. Pour the remaining cauliflower and stock in a blender and blend until smooth. In a stockpot, melt butter; sauté onion until tender. Add flour, stirring until smooth. Slowly stir in milk; blending until smooth. Stir in blended cauliflower and stock. Add Cheddar cheese; cook, stirring constantly, until sauce is smooth and cheese is melted. Add reserved cauliflower and heat until steaming. Serve garnished with parsley and Romano cheese. Makes 6 to 8 servings.

Cream of Spinach Soup

- 1½ pounds fresh spinach, washed, stems removed *or*
  - 2 10-ounce packages frozen chopped spinach
- 1 cup chopped onion
- 1 14-ounce can chicken broth
- 1 teaspoon salt
- 2 cups water
- ½ cup sour cream
- 1 tablespoon lemon juice
- ½ cup light cream
- 1 tablespoon snipped chives *or* green onions

In a large saucepan, combine spinach, onion, chicken broth, salt and water. Bring to a boil. Reduce heat and simmer, covered, 5 minutes. Blend half of the mixture in blender at low speed for 30 seconds. Return to saucepan; stir in sour cream, lemon juice and light cream. Reheat, stirring over low heat, until steaming. Serve sprinkled with chives. Makes 4 to 6 servings.

Elegant Tomato Soup

- 1 10-ounce can tomato soup
- 1 10-ounce can beef bouillon
- ½ cup Burgundy

In a stockpot, combine all ingredients. Heat to steaming. Makes 4 servings.

Cream of Tomato Soup

- 1 small onion
- 4 whole cloves
- 2 8-ounce cans tomato puree
- 1 cup water
- 1 bay leaf
- ½ teaspoon allspice
- 1 teaspoon celery salt
- ½ teaspoon salt
- 1 teaspoon sugar
- 2 cups light cream

Stud onion with whole cloves. In a large pot, combine all ingredients except cream. Bring to a boil; reduce heat and simmer for 45 minutes. Remove bay leaf and onion. Just before serving, heat cream to boiling and beat slowly into the tomato broth. Correct seasonings and serve. Makes 6 to 8 servings.

Note: To retain bright red color, do not cook in an aluminum pan.

Cream of Celery and Zucchini Soup

- 2 tablespoons butter or margarine
- 6 ribs celery, sliced
- 2 green onions, chopped
- 1 unpeeled, sliced zucchini
- 1 cup water
- 1 tablespoon instant chicken bouillon
- 1½ cups milk
- 1 tablespoon cornstarch
  - Salt
  - Pepper

In a stockpot, melt butter; sauté celery and onions until tender, but not brown. Add zucchini, water, and bouillon; cover and simmer for 10 minutes. Blend cornstarch with a little of the milk until smooth; add, stirring, to mix. Stir in remaining milk. Cook, stirring constantly, until thickened and bubbly. Season to taste with salt and pepper. Makes 4 servings.

Cream of Broccoli Soup

- ½ cup chicken broth
- 1 package frozen chopped broccoli
- 1 10-ounce can cream of celery soup
- 1 soup can milk
  - Lemon slices

In a small saucepan, bring chicken broth to a boil. Add broccoli and cook about 8 minutes, or until tender. In blender, combine broccoli, broth, soup and milk. Blend until smooth. Serve hot or chilled, garnished with lemon slices. Makes 4 servings.

Beet Borscht I

Cold Beet Soup

    8 beets, washed, peeled, halved
    1 onion, finely chopped
    2 quarts water
    1 tablespoon salt
    1 teaspoon lemon juice
    2 tablespoons sugar
    ¼ cup lemon juice
    2 eggs
      Sour cream

In a stockpot, combine beets, onion, water, salt, and 1 teaspoon lemon juice. Bring to a boil; simmer over medium heat for 1 hour. Add remaining lemon juice and sugar; simmer an additional 20 minutes. Cool. Remove beets; chop or grate them and set aside. In a large bowl, beat eggs lightly. Gradually add 2 to 3 cups soup, beating constantly to avoid curdling. Return this mixture to the remaining soup. Stir in chopped or grated beets and refrigerate until thoroughly chilled. Serve with sour cream whipped into the soup or a spoonful dropped into each bowl. Makes 6 to 8 servings.

Beet Borscht II

    2 1-pound cans diced beets and juice
    1 10-ounce can beef bouillon
    4 green onions and tops, minced
    7 radishes, sliced
    ½ cucumber, peeled and sliced
    2 tablespoons lemon juice
    1 large dill pickle, minced
    2 potatoes, cooked and sliced
      Sour cream

Combine first 6 ingredients; mix well. Refrigerate until thoroughly chilled. Serve garnished with a dollop of sour cream, topped with potato slices and dill pickle bits. Makes 6 to 8 servings.

Sugar-Free Beet Borscht

    2 1-pound cans diced beets, drained, reserve liquid
    2 cans water
      Artificial sweetener to equal 6 teaspoons sugar
    3 tablespoons lemon juice
    1 tablespoon vinegar
    1 teaspoon salt
    1 slice lemon
    1 cup sour cream

In a large pan, combine beet liquid, water, sweetener, lemon juice, vinegar, salt and lemon. Bring to a boil; reduce heat and simmer for 10 minutes. Add beets and simmer an additional 2 or 3 minutes. Refrigerate until cold. Pour off beet liquid. In blender, combine beet liquid and sour cream; blend thoroughly. Pour liquid back into beets; stir. Serve in glass bowls. Makes 8 servings.

Cold, Fresh Tomato Soup

Chill bowls before serving.

    11 large tomatoes, peeled, seeded and chopped
     1 tablespoon chopped parsley
     2 green onions, chopped
     1 teaspoon salt
     1 tablespoon sugar
     1 teaspoon basil
     2 cups light cream

In a blender, combine all ingredients except cream; blend until smooth. Refrigerate until chilled. Just before serving, stir in cream. Makes 4 to 6 servings.

Cream of Watercress Soup

    2 tablespoons butter
    1 cup chopped watercress
    ½ cup chicken broth
    3 cups light cream
    2 tablespoons white wine
      Whole watercress leaves for garnish

In a saucepan, melt butter; sauté watercress for 2 to 3 minutes. Stir in broth, cream and wine. Heat to steaming, or chill for a cold soup. Serve garnished with whole watercress leaves. Makes 4 to 6 servings.

Cold Shrimp Bisque

Elegant.

    1 10½-ounce can cream of shrimp soup
    1 cup light cream
    ½ cup tomato juice
    ⅓ cup dry sherry
      Minced dillweed
    4 cooked shrimp

In a saucepan combine soup, cream and tomato juice. Bring to a boil, stirring constantly. Reduce heat. Add sherry and simmer for a few minutes. Refrigerate several hours or overnight. Stir well before serving. Garnish each serving with dillweed and a whole shrimp. Makes 4 servings.

Gazpacho I

Cold Spanish soup, crunchy and refreshing.

- 4 cups cold chicken broth
- 2 tablespoons olive oil
- 3 tablespoons lemon or lime juice
- 2 cups tomato juice
- ½ teaspoon salt
- ½ teaspoon pepper
- ½ teaspoon sugar
- 1 small onion, minced *or* 2 green onions, chopped
- 1 cucumber, chopped
- 2 large ripe tomatoes, peeled and chopped
- ½ cup croutons

In blender, combine chicken broth, oil, lemon juice, tomato juice, salt, pepper, and sugar. Puree until smooth. Combine with vegetables. Refrigerate for an hour or so. Just before serving, garnish with croutons. Makes 8 to 10 servings.

Gazpacho II

So filling for calorie watchers.

- 2 28-ounce cans tomatoes
- 2 tablespoons wine vinegar
- ¼ teaspoon dry mustard
- ½ teaspoon salt
- ¼ teaspoon freshly ground pepper
- ¼ teaspoon sugar
- 1 cucumber, peeled, seeded and diced
- 1 green pepper, diced
- 3 tablespoons minced onion
- 3 ribs of celery, diced
- 2 tablespoons sweet pickle relish
  Tabasco sauce to taste

Drain tomatoes; reserve juice. In blender combine tomatoes, vinegar, mustard, salt, pepper and sugar, and blend until tomatoes are in small bits. In large container, combine with tomato juice, cucumber, green pepper, onion, celery, and relish. Stir in a drop or two of Tabasco sauce. Refrigerate several hours. Serve cold in glass bowls, cups or mugs. Makes 6 to 8 servings.

Chilled Cucumber and Potato Soup

- 2 cups chicken stock
- 2 medium potatoes, peeled and diced
- 2 cucumbers, peeled, seeds removed, diced
- 1 tablespoon diced onion
- 2 cups milk
- 1 cup light cream
- ½ cup sour cream
- ½ cup snipped chives

Cook potatoes in chicken stock; cool. In blender or food processor, combine potatoes, stock, cucumbers and onion. Blend until smooth. Stir in milk, cream and sour cream. Chill until icy cold. Serve garnished with chives. Makes 6 to 8 servings.

Cucumber Yogurt Soup

- 2 cucumbers, peeled, cut in chunks
- 1 teaspoon salt
- 1 clove garlic, minced
- 2 teaspoons vinegar
- 1 tablespoon fresh dill, snipped
- 1½ tablespoons fresh mint, snipped
- 2 cups yogurt
- ⅓ cup water

In blender, combine all ingredients; puree. Refrigerate 3 to 4 hours. Serve topped with fresh dill. Makes 6 servings.

Blender Beet Borscht

Whirl together in a flash.

- 1 10-ounce can beef consommé
- 1 1-pound can beets, chilled
- 1 small onion, chopped
- ½ cup sour cream
  Pepper to taste
  Sour cream to garnish

Place first 5 ingredients in a blender. Blend until smooth. Chill and serve garnished with sour cream. Makes 4 servings.

Cold Cucumber Soup

- 2 cucumbers, seeded and chopped
- 3 green onions, chopped
- 2 cups cold chicken stock
- 2 teaspoons dillweed
- ½ teaspoon salt
- 1 cup sour half and half

Combine all ingredients in blender; whirl until smooth. Serve icy cold. Makes 4 to 6 servings.

Avocado Soup

- 2 ripe avocados, peeled, pit removed
- 2 tablespoons lemon juice
- ⅛ teaspoon ginger
- 1 teaspoon salt
- ⅛ teaspoon pepper
- 3 cups milk

Cut avocado into chunks and place in blender with lemon juice and seasonings. Blend, adding milk gradually. Place plastic wrap directly on surface of soup to prevent discoloration. Refrigerate several hours or overnight. Makes 4 to 6 servings.

Chilled Soup

Vichyssoise

- 2 tablespoons butter
- 2 leeks (white part only), minced
- 1 onion, minced
- 4 potatoes, peeled, thinly sliced
- 4 cups chicken stock
- 2 cups light cream
- ½ cup chopped chives

In a stockpot, melt butter; sauté leeks and onion until tender, but not golden. Add potatoes and chicken stock; simmer for 20 minutes or until vegetables are tender. Pour into blender and blend until smooth. Pour into large container and stir in cream. Cover and refrigerate until chilled. Serve garnished with chives. Makes 6 to 8 servings.

Chilled Zucchini Soup

- ¼ cup butter or margarine
- 1 cup chopped leek
- 1 cup chopped onion
- 1 cup pared and cubed potatoes
- 1 14-ounce can chicken broth
- 2 pounds zucchini, unpeeled, thinly sliced
- 1 cup milk
- 1 teaspoon dillweed *or* 1 tablespoon chopped fresh dill
- ⅛ teaspoon crushed tarragon
  Dash white pepper
- 1 cup light cream
  Chives or dill

In a stockpot, melt butter; sauté leek and onion until tender, but not brown. Add potato and chicken broth. Bring to a boil; reduce heat and simmer, covered, 20 minutes. Add zucchini and simmer, covered, an additional 10 minutes or until potato is tender. Remove from heat. Pour mixture 2 cups at a time into blender or food processor and blend until smooth. Pour into storage container. Scald milk; slowly stir into zucchini mixture. Add dill, tarragon and pepper. Stir in cream. Refrigerate, covered, 6 hours or overnight. Serve sprinkled with chives or dill. Makes 10 to 12 servings.

Chilled Cream of Asparagus Soup

- 1 10-ounce package frozen, cut asparagus
- 1 10½-ounce can cream of asparagus soup
- 1¼ cups milk
- ¼ cup sour cream
- ½ teaspoon salt
- ¼ teaspoon pepper
  Pinch crushed basil

In a small saucepan, bring ½ cup water to a boil. Add asparagus and simmer, covered, for 5 minutes; drain. Place in blender along with remaining ingredients and blend at high speed for 2 minutes, or until smooth. Refrigerate, covered, several hours or overnight. Serve, garnished with a dollop of sour cream. Makes 4 servings.

Jellied Clam Consommé

Elegant first course for any special occasion.

- 2 envelopes unflavored gelatin
- 1½ cups cold Fish Stock (Recipe on page 4)
- 1 cup dry white wine
- 1 small onion, minced
- 2 6½-ounce cans minced clams, reserve liquid
- ½ cup lemon juice
- 1 tablespoon capers
  Tabasco sauce
  Sour cream
  Red or black caviar
  Lemon wedges

Soften gelatin in ½ cup of the fish stock. Heat wine, remaining stock and onions to boiling. Reduce heat and simmer for 5 minutes. Remove from heat. Add gelatin and stir until dissolved. Add clams with liquid, lemon juice, capers and a few drops of Tabasco. Refrigerate until set. Spoon into serving dishes. Garnish with a dollop of sour cream, a spoonful of caviar and lemon wedges. Makes 8 to 10 servings.

New Potato Vichyssoise

- 2 tablespoons margarine or butter
- 1 cup chopped green onion
- 4 cups thinly sliced new potatoes
- 3 cups chicken broth
  Dash nutmeg
  Dash white pepper
- 2 cups milk
- 1½ cups light cream
  Chopped chives

In a stockpot, melt butter; sauté onion until tender, but not brown. Add potatoes, broth, nutmeg and pepper. Bring to a boil; reduce heat and simmer 20 to 30 minutes. Pour into blender and blend until smooth. Pour into large container; add milk and cream. Cover and refrigerate until chilled. Top each serving with chives. Makes 8 servings.

Blueberry Soup

    1 21-ounce can blueberry pie filling
    ½ cup dry sherry
    ¼ cup lemon juice
    ½ cup cold water
    1 cup sour cream
       Dash cinnamon
       Dash salt

Combine all ingredients in blender and mix on high speed for 1 minute. Cover and refrigerate 3 hours or more. Serve in chilled soup bowls. Serve with hot muffins or biscuits. Makes 6 servings.

Pumpkin Soup I

    4 tablespoons butter or margarine
    1 small onion, diced
    1½ pounds pumpkin, peeled and diced or 1½-pound
       can pumpkin
    4 cups chicken stock
    ½ teaspoon salt
    2 tablespoons flour
    ¾ cup light cream, heated
       Toasted croutons
       Whipped cream

In a stockpot, melt 2 tablespoons of the butter. Sauté onion until tender, but not brown. Add pumpkin, chicken stock and salt. Simmer until pumpkin is soft. Knead flour with remaining 2 tablespoons butter; add to pumpkin mixture and bring to a boil. Pour soup into blender or processor and blend until smooth. Return soup to heat and bring to the boiling point; add light cream. Serve garnished with croutons and whipped cream. Makes 4 to 6 servings.

Pumpkin Soup II

    1 tablespoon butter or margarine
    2 tablespoons minced onion
    1 1-pound can pumpkin
    2 cups chicken broth
    ½ teaspoon salt
    ½ teaspoon mace (optional)
    1 cup light cream
    ½ cup dry sherry

In a large saucepan, melt butter; sauté onion until tender, but not brown. Add pumpkin, broth, and spices, blending well. Simmer 10 minutes. Cool slightly; slowly stir in cream and wine. Heat again to serving temperature and serve immediately. Makes 6 to 8 servings.

Lemon-Buttermilk Soup

    4 egg yolks
    ½ cup sugar
    1 tablespoon lemon juice
    2 teaspoons grated lemon peel
    1 teaspoon vanilla
    1 quart buttermilk
    8 thin slices lemon

In a blender, blend egg yolks with sugar until thick. Add lemon juice, peel and vanilla. With blender at low speed, gradually add buttermilk. Pour into a storage container and refrigerate for 3 hours or overnight. Garnish each serving with a slice of lemon. Makes 8 servings.

Cherry Potage

    1 30-ounce can dark sweet cherries, pitted
    1 14-ounce jar cranberry-orange relish
    ½ teaspoon nutmeg
    ½ cup cold water
    1 tablespoon lemon juice
       Cinnamon sticks (optional)

Combine cherries and relish in a blender. Blend on high speed for 1 minute. Stir in nutmeg, water and lemon juice, mixing well. Cover and refrigerate for 3 hours or more. Serve in chilled mugs with cinnamon sticks, if desired. Makes 6 servings.

Iced Cherry Soup

A lovely cooler!

    2 cups sour pitted cherries
    5½ cups water
    ½ cup sugar
    ½ lemon, thinly sliced
    1 stick cinnamon
    3 tablespoons cornstarch
    ½ teaspoon salt
    ½ teaspoon almond extract
    ½ teaspoon red food coloring
    1 cup sour cream

In a stockpot, mash cherries slightly. Add 5 cups of the water, sugar, lemon slices and cinnamon. Cover and cook slowly for 30 minutes. Dissolve cornstarch in remaining ½ cup water and add to cherry mixture with salt, extract and food coloring. Cook until soup clears and begins to thicken. Serve cold with a generous dollop of sour cream on each portion. Makes 4 to 6 servings.

Salads

Turn over a new leaf, or lots of them, in salad making, discovering new tastes, new textures, and new combinations. Salad may be served as a separate course (after the main dish if serving wine), with the main dish, as an appetizer, or as a main dish. For drama, mix it and toss it at the table.

What to buy:
Iceberg or head lettuce
Bibb and Boston lettuce
Romaine or leaf lettuce
Chicory, escarole, Belgian endive
Spinach
Watercress
Cabbage: celery, white, and red

How to buy
Look for fresh, crisp greens and avoid anything wilted.

How to store
Most greens will keep unwashed for a week in the crisper section of your refrigerator or in plastic bags.

How to clean
Wash well; spin dry in a salad spinner, wire basket, or layer leaves between paper towels.

How to prepare
Tear leaves and store in a plastic bag until time to eat. Pour dressing over just before serving.

Additions
Radishes, mushrooms, tomatoes, green peppers, carrots, onions, artichokes, green beans, cauliflowerets, fresh or drained canned fruits.

The Salad Bowl

Anchovy-Artichoke Salad

Lettuce leaves
1 6-ounce jar marinated artichoke hearts, drained
1 2-ounce can anchovy fillets, drained
1 4-ounce jar pimientos, drained and sliced
1 tablespoon salad oil
1 tablespoon vinegar

Arrange lettuce leaves on 6 salad plates. Arrange artichoke hearts, anchovies and pimientos attractively on top. Chill. Just before serving, combine oil and vinegar and pour over each salad. Makes 6 servings.

Wilted Lettuce Salad

4 slices bacon
¼ cup vinegar
1 teaspoon salt
¼ teaspoon freshly ground pepper
2 tablespoons sugar or sugar substitute
8 cups lettuce, torn in bite-size pieces
½ medium onion, thinly sliced

Fry bacon until crisp; drain and crumble. To bacon drippings, add vinegar, salt, pepper and sugar; heat to boiling. Pour over lettuce and onion; toss lightly and serve immediately. Makes 8 servings.

Antipasto Salad

Amount of vegetables depends on individual taste and the number of people served.

Romaine lettuce leaves
Carrots, canned; or fresh, slightly cooked
Whole green beans, canned; or fresh, slightly cooked
Tomato slices
Artichoke hearts, drained
Salami, sliced
Mozzarella cheese, sliced
Mushrooms, sliced
Red onions, thinly sliced
Hard-boiled eggs, quartered

Line a large platter with lettuce leaves. Attractively arrange remaining ingredients on top of lettuce. Serve with the following dressing.

Dressing

1 cup mayonnaise
¼ cup milk
2 tablespoons red wine vinegar
1 clove garlic, minced
¼ teaspoon oregano
¼ teaspoon basil
⅛ teaspoon pepper

Combine all ingredients, blending well. Refrigerate until serving time. Makes 1½ cups.

The Salad Bowl

Caesar Salad for the Low-Cholesterol Diet

    3 tablespoons margarine
    ¼ teaspoon garlic powder
    1½ cups bread cubes
    8 cups romaine, torn in bite-size pieces
    4 cups Boston lettuce, torn in bite-size pieces
    ⅔ cup Garlic French Dressing
    ¼ cup egg substitute
       Dash Worcestershire sauce
    2 ounces anchovy fillets, drained and cut up

Melt margarine in skillet; stir in garlic powder. Add bread cubes and sauté until golden; drain on paper towels. In a large salad bowl, combine romaine and lettuce. Pour on dressing, egg substitute, Worcestershire sauce, anchovies and bread cubes. Toss lightly until mixed well and serve. Makes 10 servings.

Garlic French Dressing

    ½ teaspoon salt
    ⅛ teaspoon freshly ground pepper
    ¼ teaspoon sugar
    ⅛ teaspoon dry mustard
    1 clove garlic, minced
    1 tablespoon water
    3 tablespoons white vinegar
    ½ cup corn oil

Combine all ingredients in jar and shake well until thoroughly blended. Makes ⅔ cup.

Green Goddess Salad
Green Goddess Dressing

    ¾ cup mayonnaise
    ¼ cup sour cream
    ¼ cup tarragon vinegar
    6 anchovy fillets, chopped
    ¼ cup chopped parsley
    2 tablespoons finely chopped green onion
    ½ teaspoon dry mustard
    ⅛ teaspoon freshly ground pepper

Combine all ingredients, blending well. Refrigerate several hours or overnight.

Salad

    8 cups romaine or other salad greens, torn in bite-size pieces
    3 cups cubed cooked turkey or chicken
       Tomato slices or cherry tomatoes

Place greens and turkey or chicken in salad bowl. Add dressing and toss lightly. Garnish with tomatoes. Makes 8 servings.

Fresh Garden Julienne

    2 cups water
    1 teaspoon salt
    ¾ pound fresh green beans, cut in half lengthwise and cut in 2-inch pieces
    ½ pound large mushrooms, sliced
    1 carrot, peeled and julienned
    1 turnip, peeled and julienned

In a medium-size saucepan, combine water and salt. Heat; add beans and bring to boil. Reduce heat and simmer, uncovered, for 15 minutes or until tender-crisp. Drain. Pour one-half of the Dressing over warm beans. Cover and refrigerate for 3 hours, tossing occasionally. Drain beans and discard liquid. In a serving bowl, combine beans, mushrooms, carrot and turnip strips. Pour remaining Dressing over all and toss gently. Makes 6 servings.

Dressing

    ⅔ cup salad or olive oil
    ¼ cup dry sherry
    1 tablespoon white wine vinegar
    ½ teaspoon salt
    ¼ teaspoon pepper
    ½ teaspoon sugar
    ½ teaspoon dry mustard

Combine all ingredients in a jar. Shake well.

Salad Bowl Italiano

    2 red onions, thinly sliced, separated into rings
    ½ cup mushrooms, sliced
    5 cups iceberg lettuce, torn into bite-size pieces
    4 cups romaine lettuce, torn into bite-size pieces
    2 cups unpeeled, thinly sliced zucchini
    ½ cup sliced radishes

In a storage container, combine onion and mushrooms. Pour Dressing Marinade over and refrigerate, covered, 3 hours or overnight. In a large salad bowl, combine greens, zucchini and radish slices. Pour onion, mushrooms and marinade over top. Toss lightly and serve. Makes 6 to 8 servings.

Dressing Marinade

    4 ounces blue cheese, crumbled
    ½ cup salad oil
    2 tablespoons lemon juice
    ½ teaspoon sugar
    ½ teaspoon salt
       Dash freshly ground pepper
       Dash paprika

Combine all ingredients in a jar. Shake well.

Oriental Mushroom Salad

With a subtle hint of ginger.

- ½ cup salad oil
- ½ cup lemon juice
- 3 tablespoons soy sauce
- 1 clove garlic, minced
- ¼ teaspoon ginger
  Dash pepper
- 1 pound fresh mushrooms, sliced
- 1 9-ounce package frozen French-style green beans, cooked tender-crisp
- 1 6-ounce package frozen pea pods, cooked tender-crisp
- ½ pound fresh bean sprouts
- 1 8-ounce can sliced water chestnuts, drained

In a jar, combine oil, lemon juice, soy sauce, garlic, ginger and pepper. Shake well. In a bowl, combine mushrooms, beans, pea pods, sprouts, and water chestnuts. Pour dressing over; toss lightly. Cover and refrigerate several hours. Makes 6 servings.

Romaine Salad

- 8 cups romaine, torn in bite-size pieces
- ½ cup (4-ounce jar) pimiento, drained and sliced
- 1 teaspoon sugar
- ½ teaspoon salt
  Dash cinnamon
- ¼ cup salad oil
- ¼ cup lemon juice

Combine romaine and pimiento in a large salad bowl. In a small jar, combine sugar, salt, cinnamon, oil and lemon juice. Shake well and pour over romaine and pimiento. Toss lightly. Makes 4 to 6 servings.

Bibb Lettuce Salad

- ¼ cup red wine vinegar
- 1 teaspoon minced chives
- ½ teaspoon salt
- ¼ teaspoon freshly ground pepper
- ½ teaspoon Worcestershire sauce
- ¼ teaspoon Dijon mustard
- 1 clove garlic, minced
- ¾ cup olive oil
- 3 heads Bibb lettuce, torn in bite-size pieces

In a mixing bowl, combine first 7 ingredients. Gradually add oil, beating until mixture is slightly thickened. Refrigerate, covered, 1 hour. Arrange Bibb lettuce on 6 plates and pour dressing over to coat lightly. Makes 6 servings.

Spinach Salad

- 1 egg
- 1 tablespoon grated Parmesan cheese
- ½ teaspoon salt
- ¼ teaspoon pepper
- 2 tablespoons Dijon mustard
- 3 tablespoons lemon juice
- 1 teaspoon Worcestershire sauce
- ½ teaspoon sugar or sugar substitute
- ¼ cup salad oil
- 1 pound spinach, stems removed, washed and dried
- 2 hard-boiled eggs, chopped
- 4 slices bacon, cooked and crumbled

Beat together egg, cheese, salt, pepper, mustard, lemon juice, Worcestershire sauce and sugar. Gradually beat in oil, blending well. Pour into a covered jar and refrigerate. At serving time, tear spinach into bite-size pieces. In a large salad bowl, combine spinach, eggs and bacon; pour on dressing and toss lightly. Makes 6 servings.

German Spinach Salad with Sweet-Sour Dressing

- 1 pound spinach, stems removed, washed and dried
- 6 slices bacon
- ½ cup cider vinegar
- ½ cup water
- 3 tablespoons sugar
- 1 teaspoon salt
- ⅛ teaspoon pepper

Tear spinach into bite-size pieces; place in a large salad bowl. Fry bacon crisp; drain and crumble. To bacon drippings, add vinegar, water, sugar, salt and pepper. Heat to boiling. Pour over spinach; toss lightly. Sprinkle with crumbled bacon and serve. Makes 6 to 8 servings.

Watercress Salad

- 2 to 3 bunches watercress, leaves only
- 16 cherry tomatoes
- 3 tablespoons olive oil
- 1 tablespoon lemon juice
- ½ teaspoon Dijon mustard
- 1 clove garlic, minced
  Salt and pepper to taste

Wash and dry watercress leaves and tomatoes. Place in a bowl. Combine remaining ingredients in a jar and shake well. Pour over salad; toss lightly. Makes 4 servings.

The Salad Bowl

Oriental Spinach Salad

- 1 pound spinach, stems removed, washed, dried and torn into bite-size pieces
- 1 can bean sprouts, drained
- 1 can sliced water chestnuts, drained
- 2 hard-boiled eggs, sliced for garnish

Combine all ingredients in a large salad bowl. Pour Dressing over and toss lightly. Garnish with egg slices. Makes 6 servings.

Dressing

- 1 cup salad oil
- ¼ cup sugar
- ⅓ cup catsup
- ¼ cup vinegar
- 1 tablespoon Worcestershire sauce
- 2 teaspoons soy sauce
- 1 small onion, grated

Combine all ingredients in a jar and shake well. Refrigerate until serving time.

Spinach, Orange and Onion Salad

- 1 pound fresh spinach, torn in bite-size pieces
- 2 large oranges, peeled, sliced; cut slices in half
- 1 large sweet onion, thinly sliced, separated into rings
- 6 slices bacon, cooked crisp, cut in large pieces

In a large salad bowl, combine all ingredients. Refrigerate until serving time. Pour Dressing over salad, toss, and serve. Makes 8 servings.

Dressing

- 2 tablespoons cider vinegar
- 1 tablespoon sugar
- 1 teaspoon salt
- ¼ teaspoon dry mustard
- ⅓ cup salad oil

Combine all ingredients in a jar and shake well.

Marinated Mushroom-Spinach Salad

When flavor really counts.

- ½ cup salad oil
- ¼ cup white wine vinegar
- ½ teaspoon basil
- ¾ teaspoon salt
- ¼ teaspoon freshly ground pepper
- 1 small onion, thinly sliced
- ½ pound mushrooms, sliced
- 1 pound spinach, stems removed, torn in bite-size pieces

Combine oil, vinegar, basil, salt and pepper, blending well. Pour over onion and mushrooms and let stand at room temperature 2 hours or refrigerate overnight. Stir occasionally. Place spinach in salad bowl; add mushroom mixture and toss well. Serve immediately. Makes 6 servings.

Caesar Salad

- ¾ cup olive oil
- 1 cup French bread cubes
- 1 clove garlic
- 2 tablespoons lemon juice
- 1 teaspoon Worcestershire sauce
- 1 teaspoon salt
- ¼ teaspoon freshly ground pepper
- 2 bunches of romaine, torn in bite-size pieces
- 2 ounces anchovy fillets, drained and chopped
- 1 egg, coddled 1 minute
- ½ cup grated Parmesan cheese

In a skillet, heat ¼ cup of the oil; sauté bread cubes with garlic until golden. Drain croutons on paper towels; discard garlic. Combine ½ cup oil, lemon juice, Worcestershire sauce, salt and pepper, mixing well. Pour over romaine. Add anchovies and toss. Add egg and toss again. Sprinkle with Parmesan and croutons; toss lightly and serve at once. Makes 6 servings.

Greek Salad

- 1 can anchovy fillets, drained, save oil
  Olive oil
- ¼ cup wine vinegar
- 1 bay leaf
- 1 clove garlic
- 1 teaspoon oregano
- ¼ cup chopped parsley
- 1 bunch romaine, torn into bite-size pieces
- ½ head lettuce, torn into bite-size pieces
- 4 endive leaves
- 2 red onions, thinly sliced
- 2 tomatoes, quartered
- 1 cucumber, scored and sliced
- ½ green pepper, cut in strips
- 8 to 10 Greek olives
- ¼ to ½ pound feta cheese, crumbled
- 4 hard-cooked eggs, quartered

Combine reserved anchovy oil and olive oil to equal ½ cup. In a jar, combine oils, vinegar, bay leaf, garlic and oregano. Shake well and chill several hours or overnight. In a large salad bowl, combine parsley, remaining vegetables, anchovy fillets and cheese. Before serving, remove bay leaf and garlic from dressing; shake well and pour over salad. Makes 4 to 6 servings.

The Salad Bowl

Mushroom Caesar Salad

- 3 anchovy fillets
- ½ pound mushrooms, thinly sliced
- ½ cup salad oil
- 2 tablespoons lemon juice
- 1 teaspoon Worcestershire sauce
- 1 clove garlic, minced
- ½ teaspoon salt
- ⅛ teaspoon freshly ground pepper
- 1 bunch romaine, torn in bite-size pieces
- 1 cup croutons
- ¼ cup grated Parmesan cheese
- 1 egg

Mash anchovies in a wooden salad bowl; add mushrooms. In a small mixing bowl, combine oil, lemon juice, Worcestershire sauce, garlic, salt and pepper, blending well. Pour over mushrooms; toss to coat well. Add romaine, croutons and cheese; toss lightly. Add egg and toss until egg is no longer visible. Serve immediately. Makes 6 servings.

Beet and Cucumber Salad

- 1 16-ounce can sliced beets, drained
- 1 cucumber, peeled, sliced
- ½ cup salad oil
- 2 tablespoons white wine vinegar
- 1 teaspoon dried, crushed tarragon leaves
- 1 teaspoon dry mustard
- ½ teaspoon salt
- ¼ teaspoon dried dillweed
- ¼ teaspoon sugar
  Lettuce leaves
- 2 hard-boiled eggs, chopped

Arrange beet and cucumber slices in overlapping rows on platter. In a jar, combine oil, vinegar, tarragon, mustard, salt, dillweed and sugar. Shake well. Pour dressing over beets and cucumbers. Refrigerate at least 1 hour. Arrange lettuce around edges of platter and sprinkle chopped egg over top. Makes 6 servings.

Asparagus and Salad Vinaigrette

- 3 tablespoons tarragon vinegar
- ¼ cup salad oil
- 2 tablespoons olive oil
- ½ teaspoon sugar
  Salt and pepper to taste
- 2½ pounds asparagus, cooked until just tender
  Lettuce leaves
- 1 hard-boiled egg, chopped
- 2 tablespoons sweet pickle relish
- 2 tablespoons chopped parsley

Combine first 5 ingredients in a jar and shake well to blend. Pour dressing over warm asparagus and refrigerate for 1 hour, turning asparagus several times. Serve on lettuce-lined plates and garnish with chopped egg, relish and parsley. Makes 6 servings.

Artichoke Heart Salad

- 4 cups salad greens, torn into bite-size pieces
- 2 tomatoes, chopped
- 2 6-ounce jars marinated artichoke hearts with liquid
- 2 tablespoons lemon juice

In a serving bowl, combine all ingredients. Toss lightly and serve. Makes 4 to 6 servings.

Mixed Vegetable Salad

- ¾ cup cider vinegar
- ½ cup salad oil
- 2 tablespoons sugar
- 1 teaspoon salt
- ¼ teaspoon freshly ground pepper
- 2 16-ounce cans whole kernel corn, drained
- ½ head cauliflower, cut into flowerets
- 1 medium red onion, thinly sliced

In a storage container, combine vinegar, oil, sugar, salt and pepper, mixing well. Add remaining ingredients and toss gently to coat vegetables. Cover and refrigerate 4 hours or overnight, tossing several times. Toss salad before serving. Makes 8 servings.

Cauliflower Salad

- 4 cups raw, sliced cauliflower
- 1 cup coarsely chopped ripe olives
- ½ cup chopped green pepper
- ¼ cup chopped pimiento
- ½ cup chopped onion
- ½ cup salad or olive oil
- 3 tablespoons lemon juice
- 3 tablespoons wine vinegar
- 2 teaspoons salt
- ¼ teaspoon freshly ground pepper
- ½ teaspoon sugar
  Crisp salad greens to line bowl

In a large storage bowl, combine cauliflower, olives, green pepper, pimiento and onion. In a small mixing bowl, beat together oil, lemon juice, vinegar and seasonings, blending well. Pour dressing over vegetables; cover and refrigerate 3 hours or overnight. Toss just before serving in a large bowl lined with crisp greens. Makes 8 to 10 servings.

Tomato Salad

Brighten a warm-weather menu.

Lettuce leaves
12 large tomato slices
Salt
Freshly ground pepper
1 tablespoon crushed basil
3 tablespoons red wine vinegar
½ cup olive oil

Arrange lettuce leaves on 4 individual salad plates. Arrange tomato slices on top. Sprinkle with salt, freshly ground pepper and basil. Combine vinegar and oil in a jar. Shake and pour over each. Serve immediately. Makes 4 servings.

Combination Vegetable Salad

Colorful.

3 tomatoes, coarsely chopped
3 medium onions, coarsely chopped
3 green peppers, coarsely chopped
1 tablespoon chopped parsley
1 clove garlic, minced
1 teaspoon salt
½ teaspoon freshly ground pepper
¾ cup red wine vinegar
2 tablespoons salad oil

Combine all ingredients in a large glass bowl. Chill, covered, 4 to 6 hours. Makes 8 servings.

Four-Layer Salad

6 cups (1 medium head) lettuce, torn in
  bite-size pieces
1 red onion, thinly sliced and separated into rings
2 cups cauliflower, broken into small flowerets
2 small zucchini, thinly sliced

In a glass serving bowl, layer lettuce, onion, cauliflower, and zucchini. Spread Dressing over top. Cover and refrigerate 4 to 6 hours or overnight. Makes 8 servings.

Dressing

⅓ cup mayonnaise
⅓ cup French dressing
1 tablespoon lemon juice
1 tablespoon horseradish
1 teaspoon Worcestershire sauce
4 drops Tabasco sauce
½ cup frozen non-dairy topping, thawed

Combine all ingredients except topping; blend well. Fold in topping.

Classy Cukes

4 cucumbers, peeled and sliced very thin
2 tablespoons salt
1½ cups sour cream
1 tablespoon sugar
3 tablespoons vinegar
1 medium onion, sliced very thin

Sprinkle cucumbers with salt and refrigerate for 3 hours. Rinse in cold water and squeeze out liquid. In a serving bowl, combine sour cream, sugar and vinegar, mixing well. Fold in cucumbers and onions. Chill until serving time. Makes 6 to 8 servings.

Zucchini Salad

⅓ cup salad or olive oil
2 tablespoons lemon juice
2 tablespoons white wine vinegar
1 teaspoon sugar
¾ teaspoon salt
¼ teaspoon freshly ground pepper
Crisp salad greens to line bowl
1 pound zucchini, unpeeled, cut into ½-inch slices
2 red delicious apples, unpeeled, quartered, cut into
  ½-inch slices
1 cup sliced red onion
1 green pepper, chopped
1 cup diagonally sliced celery

In a jar, combine first 6 ingredients. Shake well to mix. Line large salad bowl with crisp greens. Add remaining vegetables. Pour dressing over and toss lightly. Makes 8 to 10 servings.

French Radish Salad

6 cups thinly sliced radishes (about 2 pounds)
12 green onions, chopped
½ cup chopped parsley

In a serving bowl, combine all vegetables. Refrigerate until chilled. Just before serving, toss with Mustard Dressing. Makes 8 to 10 servings.

Mustard Dressing

6 tablespoons Dijon mustard
2 tablespoons lemon juice
2 teaspoons white wine vinegar
2 cloves garlic, minced
1 teaspoon dry mustard
¼ teaspoon freshly ground pepper
1 cup salad oil

In a small bowl, combine all ingredients except oil. Gradually pour in oil, beating with a wire whisk to blend. Cover and refrigerate 3 to 4 hours.

Layered Vegetable Salad I

No last-minute fussing with this salad; cover, chill and forget it until serving time.

 ½ head lettuce, sliced
 1 green pepper, sliced
 2 ribs celery, sliced
 ¼ pound fresh mushrooms, sliced
 1 sweet onion, chopped
 1 10-ounce package frozen peas, thawed
 1 cup mayonnaise
 1 teaspoon sugar
 ½ teaspoon salt
 ¼ teaspoon garlic powder
 ¼ teaspoon basil
 1 cup grated Cheddar cheese
 4 strips bacon, cooked crisp, crumbled

In a serving bowl with straight sides, layer lettuce, green pepper, celery, mushrooms, onion, and peas. In a mixing bowl, combine mayonnaise, sugar, salt, garlic powder and basil; mix well. Spread mixture evenly over the peas. Sprinkle with Cheddar cheese and bacon. Cover and refrigerate for at least 4 hours or overnight. To serve, spoon into salad bowl so that each serving contains all layers of the salad. Makes 6 servings.

Layered Salad II

 4 cups shredded lettuce
 12 cherry tomatoes, halved
 1 cup grated Cheddar cheese
 1 10-ounce package frozen peas, thawed
 ½ cup pecan halves
 Salad Dressing

In a straight-sided glass serving bowl, layer 2 cups of the lettuce, a row of tomatoes (cut sides against glass), cheese, peas and remaining lettuce. Cover with salad dressing; sprinkle with pecans. Refrigerate until serving time. Makes 6 servings.

Salad Dressing

 ½ cup mayonnaise
 ½ cup sour cream
 1 tablespoon lemon juice
 1 teaspoon prepared mustard
 2 tablespoons minced green onion
 1 tablespoon dillweed (optional)

In a small mixing bowl, combine all ingredients, blending well.

Garden Vegetable Salad

Summer's bounty.

 8 cups mixed salad greens, torn into pieces
 4 cups fresh garden vegetables, any combination of the following:
 tomato wedges
 red onion slices
 cucumber slices
 cauliflowerets
 carrots, julienned or sliced in thin rounds
 zucchini, unpeeled, thinly sliced
 asparagus, sliced on diagonal
 broccoli flowerets
 green beans, sliced
 mushrooms, sliced

Combine all ingredients, chill and toss with French Dressing just before serving (Recipe on page 45). Makes 6 servings.

Bean Sprout Salad

 ¼ cup olive oil
 2 tablespoons wine vinegar
 ½ teaspoon salt
 ¼ teaspoon freshly ground pepper
 ¼ cup chopped pimiento
 2 tablespoons toasted sesame seed
 1 clove garlic, minced
 3 cups bean sprouts

In a jar, combine all ingredients, except bean sprouts; shake well. Pour over bean sprouts and refrigerate for at least 1 hour. Makes 4 servings.

Fresh Mushroom Salad with Lemon French Dressing

Lemon French Dressing

 ⅔ cup olive oil
 3 tablespoons wine vinegar
 3 tablespoons fresh lemon juice
 1½ teaspoons salt
 ¾ teaspoon freshly ground pepper
 2 cloves garlic, minced

In a jar, combine all ingredients for dressing; shake well. Refrigerate 3 hours to blend flavors.

Salad

 1½ cups thinly sliced mushrooms
 12 cups mixed greens, torn in bite-size pieces
 1 cup croutons

In a large salad bowl, combine greens and mushroom slices. Bring dressing to room temperature. Pour over salad and toss lightly. Sprinkle with croutons. Makes 8 servings.

MacFrank Salad

- 1 cup elbow macaroni
- ½ pound frankfurters, cooked and sliced in rounds
- ¾ cup mayonnaise
- 1 tablespoon prepared mustard
- ½ teaspoon salt
- ¼ teaspoon pepper
- ½ cup cubed Cheddar cheese
- 2 green onions, chopped

Cook macaroni according to package directions; drain. Add remaining ingredients and toss gently. Cover and refrigerate several hours. Makes 6 to 8 servings.

Note: For variety, use cubed or julienne sandwich meat instead of frankfurters.

Basic Coleslaw

- 4 cups shredded cabbage
- 1 carrot, peeled and grated
- ½ green pepper, sliced
- ¼ cup finely chopped onion
- ½ cup mayonnaise
- ½ teaspoon sugar
- ½ teaspoon salt
- ⅛ teaspoon pepper

Prepare vegetables and place in large serving bowl. Mix together remaining ingredients, blending well. Pour over salad and toss. Makes 6 servings.

Note: For variety, stir in 1 cup chopped apple mixed with 1 tablespoon lemon juice or add ½ cup pineapple chunks.

Three-Bean Salad

- ½ cup vinegar
- ¼ cup salad oil
- 2 tablespoons sugar
- 1 teaspoon salt
- ⅛ teaspoon pepper
- 1 16-ounce can whole green beans, drained
- 1 16-ounce can whole wax beans or chick peas, drained
- 1 16-ounce can red kidney beans, drained and rinsed with cold water
- ¼ cup sliced green onion
- ¼ cup chopped green pepper

In a small bowl, combine vinegar, oil, sugar and spices, blending well. In a large storage container, combine remaining ingredients. Pour dressing over and toss lightly. Cover and refrigerate at least 4 hours or overnight. Drain and serve in a lettuce-lined bowl. Makes 8 to 10 servings.

Two-Bean Salad

- 1 16-ounce can wax beans, drained
- 1 16-ounce can red kidney beans, drained and rinsed with cold water
- 1 cup sour cream
- 1 onion, minced
- 1 tablespoon vinegar
  Salt and pepper to taste

Combine beans in a serving bowl. Blend sour cream with onion, vinegar, salt and pepper. Pour over beans; cover and refrigerate several hours. Makes 4 to 6 servings.

Macaroni Salad a la Garden

- 1 cup elbow macaroni
- 1 teaspoon salt
- ¼ teaspoon pepper
- 1 cup diced cucumber
- 1 cup sliced celery
- ¼ cup sliced green pepper
- ¼ cup sliced radishes
- ¼ cup chopped green onions
- 2 tomatoes, diced
- ¾ cup mayonnaise
- ¼ teaspoon crushed basil

Cook macaroni according to package directions; drain. Combine all ingredients and toss to mix. Cover and refrigerate several hours. Makes 6 to 8 servings.

Macaroni-Meat Salad

- 1 cup elbow macaroni
- 1 8-ounce jar pasteurized process cheese spread
- ½ pound leftover beef, ham or chicken, julienned
- 1 cup chopped celery
- ¾ cup barbecue sauce
- ¼ cup mayonnaise

Cook macaroni according to package directions; drain. Combine hot macaroni and cheese; stir until cheese melts. Add remaining ingredients, mixing well. Refrigerate several hours. Makes 6 to 8 servings.

For extra-smooth vinegar and oil dressing, place ingredients in a screw-top jar along with an ice cube. After shaking, discard the ice cube.

Potato Salad

6 medium-size boiling potatoes
1 cup finely chopped onion
⅔ cup chicken stock
⅓ cup olive oil
1 tablespoon white wine vinegar
2 teaspoons prepared mustard
1 teaspoon horseradish
2 teaspoons salt
1 teaspoon freshly ground pepper
1 tablespoon lemon juice

In a large pot, place unpeeled potatoes in enough lightly salted water to cover. Boil briskly until they show slight resistance when pierced with fork; do not overcook. Drain, peel and cut in ¼-inch slices. Tightly cover and set aside. Combine remaining ingredients, except lemon juice, in a saucepan and bring to a boil. Reduce heat, cover and simmer 5 minutes. Stir in lemon juice. Pour over potatoes and toss to mix. Cool before serving. Makes 6 servings.

Potato Salad Alfredo

This is a meal in a dish for warm weather.

6 pounds red potatoes, pared, cooked
1 pound Swiss cheese, julienned
2 cups mayonnaise
½ cup sour cream
2 teaspoons chopped chives or green onion
1 teaspoon salt
2 dashes Tabasco sauce
½ pound ham, julienned
½ green pepper, cut into strips

Slice potatoes and combine with Swiss cheese. In a small mixing bowl, mix together mayonnaise, sour cream, chives, salt and Tabasco sauce. Toss gently; cover and refrigerate 4 hours or overnight. Just before serving, arrange ham and green pepper on top. Makes 8 to 10 servings.

Hot Corned Beef and Potato Salad

1 cup corned beef, cubed or julienned
1 cup julienned carrots
¾ cup mayonnaise
¼ cup cider vinegar
2 tablespoons horseradish
¼ teaspoon pepper
2 green onions, sliced
4 cups cubed, cooked potatoes

In a large frying pan, combine all ingredients except potatoes; heat. Add potatoes, tossing to mix. Serve hot. Serves 4 to 6.

German-Style Potato Salad

4 slices bacon, cooked and crumbled, reserve drippings
Salad oil
½ cup sugar
3 tablespoons flour
2 teaspoons salt
¼ teaspoon pepper
1 cup cider vinegar
1 cup water
4 pounds salad potatoes, cooked and sliced
4 green onions, chopped

Add enough oil to bacon drippings to make ½ cup. Add sugar, flour, salt and pepper to drippings; stir until smooth. Gradually stir in vinegar and water; cook 3 minutes, stirring constantly. Pour over potatoes and onions; set aside at room temperature for 3 hours. Sprinkle with bacon and serve. Makes 10 to 12 servings.

French Potato Salad

4 pounds potatoes, boiled in skins and chilled
2 cups mayonnaise
¼ cup lemon juice
1 tablespoon salt
¼ teaspoon pepper
½ teaspoon dry mustard
1 cup chopped celery
½ cup chopped green pepper
½ cup finely chopped onion

Peel and cube potatoes. In a large serving bowl, combine mayonnaise, lemon juice, salt, pepper and mustard; mix well. Add potatoes, celery, green pepper and onion. Toss to coat well. Cover and refrigerate several hours before serving. Makes 10 servings.

Parmesan Potato Salad

4 cups cubed cooked potatoes
4 hard-boiled eggs, chopped
1 cup sliced celery
¼ cup chopped onion
¼ cup chopped green pepper
1 teaspoon salt
¼ teaspoon pepper
7 slices crispy cooked bacon, crumbled
3 ounces grated Parmesan cheese
½ cup mayonnaise or salad dressing

In a large serving dish, combine all ingredients and mix thoroughly. Makes 6 to 8 servings.

Wooden salad bowls will not become sticky if washed, dried, and then rubbed with a piece of waxed paper before using.

Beef Salad

Leftovers never tasted so good!

    3 cups cooked steak or roast beef, cut in thin strips
    2 tomatoes, cut in wedges
    1 green pepper, cut in strips
    1 cup sliced celery
    2 green onions, chopped
    ½ cup sliced fresh mushrooms
    ½ cup teriyaki sauce
    ⅓ cup dry sherry
    ⅓ cup salad oil
    3 tablespoons white or rice vinegar
    ½ teaspoon ginger
    1 cup bean sprouts
    4 cups shredded Chinese cabbage

In a large bowl, combine beef, tomatoes, green pepper, celery, onions and mushrooms. In a jar, mix teriyaki sauce, sherry, oil, vinegar and ginger; shake well. Pour dressing over beef mixture; toss lightly to coat. Cover and refrigerate 2 to 3 hours. Add bean sprouts and toss again. Line bowl or platter with shredded cabbage and top with meat mixture. Makes 6 servings.

California Shrimp Salad with Avocado Cream Dressing

    4 lettuce leaves
    24 cooked, peeled shrimp
    1 cup cottage cheese
    4 slices lemon

Arrange lettuce leaves on 4 individual salad plates. Top with a scoop (¼ cup) of cottage cheese; surround with shrimp. Garnish with a lemon twist. Serve with Avocado Cream Dressing. Makes 4 servings.

Avocado Cream Dressing

    1 large avocado, peeled and pitted
    1 cup sour cream
    1 teaspoon grated lemon peel
    1 tablespoon fresh lemon juice
    2 teaspoons prepared horseradish
    ½ teaspoon salt

In a small bowl, mash avocado. Stir in remaining ingredients, mixing well. Cover with plastic wrap placed directly on top of dressing. Refrigerate 30 minutes.

Chicken Rice Salad

    1 3-pound chicken, cut up
    1 large leek, thinly sliced
    1 cup cooked rice
    ½ cup chopped celery
    ½ cup chopped green pepper

Place chicken in enough salted water to cover. Bring to a boil; reduce heat and cover. Simmer for 1 hour or until tender. Remove chicken; set aside broth. Discard skin and bones. Cube chicken. Heat broth to boiling and cook leek for 5 minutes; drain. Combine chicken, leek, rice, celery and green pepper; mix well. Pour Dressing over and mix; refrigerate several hours before serving. Makes 6 servings.

Dressing

    ½ cup salad or olive oil
    3 tablespoons white wine vinegar
    1 egg yolk
    ½ teaspoon crushed tarragon
    ½ teaspoon dry mustard
    ½ teaspoon salt
    ¼ teaspoon pepper
    ½ teaspoon sugar
    ¼ cup heavy cream, whipped

Combine 2 tablespoons of the oil, vinegar, egg yolk and seasonings in blender. Blend at high speed for 10 seconds. Gradually add remaining oil, blending well after each addition. Fold into whipped cream.

Salad Nicoise

    ½ cup salad oil
    ¼ cup red wine vinegar
    ½ teaspoon salt
    1 clove garlic, minced
    2 hard-boiled eggs, sliced
    4 large potatoes, cooked, pared and cut into
       ½-inch slices
    1 pound fresh green beans, cooked
    1 red onion, thinly sliced
    1 tomato, cut in wedges
    1 4½-ounce can pitted black olives
    1 2-ounce can anchovy fillets, drained
    1 6½-ounce can tuna, drained and cut into chunks
    2 hard-boiled eggs, sliced

In a jar, combine oil, vinegar, salt and garlic; blend well. Set aside a few egg slices for garnish. In a large salad bowl, combine remaining ingredients. Pour dressing over; toss thoroughly. Cover and refrigerate 1 hour. Garnish with reserved egg slices. Makes 6 servings.

California Shrimp Salad
with Avocado Cream Dressing

Main Dish Salads

Tuna Chef's Salad

- 1 7-ounce can tuna packed in oil
- ¼ cup red wine vinegar
- ¼ cup sliced ripe olives
- ½ teaspoon salt
- ¼ teaspoon pepper
- 1 head lettuce, torn in bite-size pieces
- ½ green pepper, sliced
- 1 red onion, sliced in rings
- 2 tomatoes, cut in wedges
- 2 hard-boiled eggs, sliced (optional)

Coarsely flake tuna; do not drain. In a large bowl, combine tuna, vinegar, olives, salt, pepper, lettuce and green pepper. Toss lightly to mix. Arrange onion rings, tomato wedges and egg slices on top. Makes 4 servings.

Corned Beef and Cabbage Salad

- ¾ cup mayonnaise
- 2 tablespoons horseradish
- 2 tablespoons milk
- 1 tablespoon mustard
- ½ teaspoon salt
- ⅛ teaspoon pepper
- 2 cups boiled, cubed, cold potatoes
- 3 cups thinly sliced cabbage
- 1 cup grated carrot
- ½ pound corned beef, julienne sliced
- 4 ounces Swiss cheese, julienne sliced
  Cabbage leaves for lining serving bowl

In a large mixing bowl, combine first 6 ingredients and mix well. Add potatoes, cabbage and carrot; toss to coat. Line serving bowl with cabbage leaves. Fill with salad and arrange corned beef and Swiss cheese slices on top. Makes 4 servings.

Tuna, Zucchini and Caper Salad

- 1 7-ounce can tuna packed in oil
- 1 small red onion, thinly sliced
- 3 tablespoons white wine vinegar
- 2 tablespoons capers, drained
- 2 zucchini, unpeeled, thinly sliced
- ½ teaspoon salt
- ¼ teaspoon pepper
  Lettuce leaves
  Stuffed olive slices for garnish

Coarsely flake tuna; do not drain. In a large bowl, combine all ingredients except lettuce and olives. Toss lightly. Refrigerate 3 to 4 hours. To serve, line platter with lettuce leaves; spoon tuna salad on top and garnish with olive slices. Makes 4 servings.

Mock Lobster Salad

- 2 pounds frozen cod
- 1 bay leaf
- 1 tablespoon salt
- 1 tablespoon lemon juice
  Paprika
- 2 hard-boiled eggs, chopped (optional)
- 1 rib celery, thinly sliced (optional)

In a large skillet bring enough water to a boil to cover fish; add bay leaf and salt. Cut fish in chunks; add fish and lemon juice to boiling water. Return water to a boil; reduce heat slightly and simmer fish 5 minutes. Remove fish with a slotted spoon. Sprinkle with paprika. Refrigerate while preparing dressing. Pour Dressing over fish; garnish with chopped egg and celery. Makes 4 to 6 servings.

Dressing

- ⅓ cup chili sauce
- ⅔ cup mayonnaise
- 1 tablespoon sweet pickle relish
- ⅛ teaspoon dry mustard
- 1 green onion, chopped
  Dash Tabasco sauce

Combine all ingredients and stir to mix well. Refrigerate for 1 hour.

Chicken Salad Pie

- 2 envelopes unflavored gelatin
- 1 cup cold water
- 1 10-ounce can chicken broth
- 1 cup mayonnaise
- 2 tablespoons lemon juice
- ⅓ cup diced celery
- ⅓ cup diced green pepper
- ⅓ cup halved green grapes
- 2 cups diced, cooked chicken or turkey
- 1 9-inch baked pie shell, cooled
  Parsley for garnish

In a medium-size saucepan, sprinkle gelatin over water; stir, over low heat, to dissolve. Remove from heat; stir in broth, mayonnaise and lemon juice. Beat until smooth. Refrigerate, stirring occasionally, until slightly thickened. Fold in vegetables and chicken; pour into pie shell; refrigerate until firm. Garnish with parsley. Makes 6 servings.

Chicken Salad a la Soy

    1 3-pound roasting chicken
    3 tablespoons sesame oil
    3 tablespoons soy sauce
      Dash Tabasco sauce
    1 small head lettuce, shredded
      Toasted slivered almonds for garnish
      Mandarin orange slices or pineapple cubes
      for garnish

Place chicken, breast side up, in a shallow roasting pan. Roast uncovered in a 375° preheated oven for 2 hours, or until drumstick easily moves up and down in socket. Cool; discard skin and bones. Shred chicken and refrigerate. Combine oil, soy sauce and Tabasco; blend well and pour over chicken. Line a platter or individual plates with shredded lettuce. Mound chicken mixture on top. Garnish with almonds and fruit. Makes 8 servings.

Chicken or Tuna Macaroni Salad

    1 cup elbow or shell macaroni
    ¾ cup mayonnaise
    1 tablespoon lemon juice
    1 7-ounce can tuna, drained and flaked, or 1 cup
      cubed, cooked chicken or turkey
    1 green onion, chopped
    1 teaspoon salt

Cook macaroni according to package directions; drain. Combine all ingredients; toss gently to mix well. Cover and refrigerate at least 1 hour. Makes 6 servings.

Note: For variation, add 1 of the following fruits: 1 orange, cut into segments; ½ cup raisins; ½ cup pineapple tidbits.

Maryland Crab Salad

If you can't get blue crab, you may substitute Alaska crab.

    1 pound backfin crab meat
    1 rib celery, minced
    ½ cup mayonnaise
    2 tablespoons lemon juice
      Lettuce leaves

Remove cartilage from crab meat, leaving meat in chunks. Combine crab, celery, mayonnaise and lemon juice; mix gently. Serve on lettuce leaves or use to stuff tomatoes. Makes 4 servings.

Chicken Lee Salad

    3½ pounds whole chicken, cut up, or 3½ pounds
        chicken breasts
      1 head lettuce

Bring 3 quarts of water to a boil. Add chicken and boil 15 minutes. Turn off heat; leave chicken in water for 45 minutes. Remove chicken from liquid; discard skin and bones and refrigerate. Prepare Sauce. Reserve 4 to 6 lettuce leaves. Shred remainder of head. Arrange lettuce leaves on a platter; mound with shredded lettuce. Cut chilled chicken into 1 x 2-inch pieces and arrange on lettuce. Pour warm Sauce over chicken and serve. Makes 4 servings.

Sauce

    4 tablespoons soy sauce
    2 tablespoons honey
    2 cloves garlic, minced
    3 tablespoons salad oil
    6 chopped green onions
    4 slices fresh gingerroot
    ½ teaspoon crushed red chili pepper

Combine soy sauce, honey and garlic. Stir and set aside for 15 minutes. In a small saucepan, combine oil, green onion, gingerroot and chili pepper. Simmer 3 minutes. Add to soy sauce mixture, blending well. Makes ¾ to 1 cup.

Chicken Liver Salad

Protein packed.

    2 tablespoons butter
    ½ pound chicken livers
    1 tablespoon instant minced onion
      Dash garlic powder
    1 tablespoon water
    1 can water chestnuts, thinly sliced
    2 tablespoons fresh lemon juice
    ¼ cup salad oil
    1 teaspoon soy sauce
    1 teaspoon brown sugar
    1 tablespoon finely chopped candied ginger
    4 cups mixed salad greens

Melt butter in a skillet; gently sauté chicken livers until pink is gone. Set aside to cool. Stir onion and garlic powder into water. Combine water chestnuts, lemon juice, oil, soy sauce, sugar, ginger, and onion-garlic mixture. Mix well and stir into chicken livers. Toss with salad greens and serve on chilled plates. Makes 4 to 6 servings.

Fruit Salads

Fresh Fruit Salad Plate Suggestions

Choose fresh fruits to make interesting combinations of colors, shapes and flavors. For instance:

    Banana chunks dipped in lemon juice
    Apple wedges dipped in lemon juice
    Pear halves or slices dipped in lemon juice
    Peach halves or slices dipped in lemon juice
    Grapefruit segments
    Orange segments or slices
    Cherries with stems
    Strawberries, blueberries, raspberries
    Melon slices or chunks
    Small bunches of grapes
    Pineapple slices or fingers
    Pomegranate seeds

Winter Fruit Salad with Maple Cream

    2 navel oranges
    2 bananas
      Lemon juice
    1 pear, unpeeled, cut into eighths
    1 apple, unpeeled, cut into eighths
    1 20-ounce can pineapple slices, drained
    ½ pound grapes, cut into clusters
      Lettuce leaves

Peel oranges and cut into ¼-inch round slices. Peel bananas and cut in half crosswise, then lengthwise; brush with lemon juice. Arrange fruit in groups on lettuce-lined platter. Place a bowl of Maple Cream Dressing in the middle. Makes 4 to 6 servings.

Maple Cream Dressing

    1 cup sour cream
    3 tablespoons maple syrup

Stir maple syrup into sour cream, mixing well.

All Seasons Fruit Salad

    2 bananas, sliced
    2 oranges, peeled and chopped
    2 red apples, seeded and chopped
    2 pears, seeded and chopped
      Juice of one lemon
      Lettuce leaves

Prepare fruit and combine in a large bowl; squeeze lemon juice over and mix well. Arrange lettuce leaves on 6 individual salad plates. Divide fruit among plates and serve. Makes 6 servings.

Waldorf Salad

    2 cups unpeeled, chopped apples
    1 tablespoon lemon juice
    1 cup diced celery
    1 cup Tokay grapes, halved and seeded (optional)
    ½ cup coarsely chopped walnuts
    ½ cup mayonnaise
    3 tablespoons sour cream
      Lettuce leaves

In a large serving bowl, toss apples with lemon juice. Add celery, grapes, and nuts. In a small mixing bowl, combine mayonnaise with sour cream, blending well. Pour over fruit, tossing gently to mix. Serve in lettuce cups. Makes 6 to 8 servings.

Watermelon Basket

    1 watermelon
    1 pint strawberries, hulled
    1 fresh pineapple, cut into chunks
    1 honeydew melon, scooped into balls
    1 cantaloupe, cut into small pieces
    1 pound green grapes, cut into clusters

To make handle: Outline a handle by inserting wooden picks in 2 lines 1½ inches apart across the middle of the top of the watermelon. On each side of the handle, position picks around the melon to outline 4 large scallops. Cut out the two pieces from each side of the handle. Cut watermelon meat from under handle. Scoop out 3 cups of watermelon balls from inside of watermelon, removing seeds. Cut around inside of watermelon so shell is about ¾-inch thick. Fill basket with fruit. Makes 10 to 12 servings.

Chicken Pineapple Boat

    1 pineapple
    2 cups cooked, cubed chicken
    ½ cup chopped green pepper
    ½ cup sliced water chestnuts, drained
    ½ cup mayonnaise
    ¼ cup sour cream
      Split cashews

Cut pineapple in half or quarter lengthwise. Do not cut off top. Scoop out pineapple from shell; remove core and cube. Combine remaining ingredients, except cashews, with pineapple; mix well and heap into shells. Sprinkle split cashews on top. Makes 2 to 4 servings.

All Season Fruit Salad with French Dressing, 45 and Mock Creme Fraiche, 45

Fruit Salads

Cranberry-Grapefruit Salad

- 1 8-ounce can jellied cranberry sauce, chilled
- 1 8-ounce can grapefruit sections, drained and chilled
  Lettuce leaves

Slice cranberry sauce in 4 slices. Attractively arrange cranberry sauce and grapefruit sections on a lettuce-lined platter or on individual plates. Serve Dressing with salad. Makes 4 servings.

Honey Dressing

- ⅓ cup mayonnaise
- 1 tablespoon honey
- 2 teaspoons vinegar
- ¼ teaspoon celery seed

In a small bowl, combine dressing ingredients, blending well.

Strawberry-Pineapple Salad

- 4 Boston lettuce leaves
- 1 pint strawberries, washed, hulled and sliced lengthwise, reserve 4 whole strawberries
- 4 slices fresh or canned pineapple

On each individual salad plate, place a lettuce leaf and a pineapple slice on top. Arrange strawberries, petal fashion on top of pineapple and top with a whole berry. Serve with Honey Lime Dressing. Makes 4 servings.

Honey Lime Dressing

- ¾ cup mayonnaise
- 2 tablespoons honey
- 1 tablespoon grated lime rind
- 2 tablespoons fresh lime juice
  Dash ground ginger

In a small bowl, combine all ingredients and mix well.

Citrus Salad

- 2 white grapefruit, peeled and sectioned
- 2 oranges, peeled and sectioned
- 1 sweet red onion, thinly sliced, separated into rings
- 4 teaspoons salad or olive oil
- 4 teaspoons wine vinegar
- ¾ teaspoon salt
  Lettuce leaves

Combine fruit and onion in a bowl. Combine oil, vinegar and salt, mixing well. Pour dressing over fruit and onion and toss gently. Serve in a lettuce-lined glass bowl. Makes 4 servings.

Pear and Cheese Salad

- ½ cup crumbled blue cheese
- ½ cup salad oil
- 2 tablespoons lemon juice
- 1 teaspoon honey
- ½ teaspoon salt
- 4 medium pears, sliced
- 8 lettuce leaves

In a small mixing bowl, combine cheese, oil, lemon juice, honey and salt; mix well with a wire whisk. Add pears and gently turn over to coat. Arrange pears on lettuce leaves. Makes 4 to 6 servings.

Ambrosia Salad

- 1 cup orange segments
- 1 cup seedless grape halves
- 1 cup shredded coconut
- 1 cup miniature marshmallows
- 1 cup sour cream

In a small bowl, combine all ingredients, mixing well. Refrigerate several hours. Makes 6 to 8 servings.

Fruit Salad

- 1 large pineapple, rind and core removed, cut in chunks
- ¼ watermelon, rind and seeds removed, cut up
- 1 cantaloupe, rind and seeds removed, cut up
- 1 honeydew, rind and seeds removed, cut up
- 3 bananas, peeled and sliced, sprinkled with lemon juice
- 1½ pounds plums, pitted, cut in wedges
- 1 pound seedless grapes

Combine all fruits in large bowl or arrange separately on large platter. Makes 12 servings.

Papaya Salad

- 4 lettuce leaves
- 1 large papaya, peeled, quartered, seeded
- 1 large banana, sliced

Arrange lettuce on 4 salad plates. Top with papaya and sliced bananas. Pour dressing over salad. Makes 4 servings.

Dressing

- 2 tablespoons salad oil
- 3 tablespoons orange juice
- 1 teaspoon lemon juice

Combine all ingredients in a jar and shake well.

Molded Salad Tips

There are three stages in chilling gelatin:

Slightly thickened

The gelatin is chilled to the consistency of un-beaten egg whites. At this stage, gently fold in fruit, vegetables, meat or seafood so that the food will remain suspended in the gelatin.

Almost firm

A mold will gel in 2 distinct layers if the first layer is chilled until "almost firm." At this stage, gelatin is tacky to the touch. Slowly spoon the second layer over the "almost firm" layer.

Firm

When the mold is completely set and firm to the touch, it is ready to be unmolded.

Unmolding

Lightly oil the mold before filling. When gelatin is firm, loosen the edges with a spatula. Place serving plate upside down on top of the mold. Invert plate and mold and shake gently until the gelatin falls out. Lift off the mold and garnish as desired. If the gelatin does not drop out easily, dip mold in warm water up to the rim for a few seconds and proceed as above.

Tuna Mold

    1 envelope unflavored gelatin
1¾ cups milk
    2 egg yolks
    1 teaspoon salt
¼ teaspoon pepper
    1 7-ounce can tuna, drained and flaked
    1 teaspoon prepared mustard
    2 tablespoons lemon juice
½ cup chopped celery
    2 tablespoons chopped pimiento
      Tomato slices for garnish

In a saucepan, stir gelatin into ½ cup of the milk. Beat together egg yolks, remaining milk, salt and pepper. Add to gelatin mixture and heat, stirring constantly, until gelatin is dissolved. Remove from heat and refrigerate until slightly thickened. Combine tuna, mustard, lemon juice, celery and pimiento; fold into gelatin mixture. Pour into a 3-cup oiled ring mold and refrigerate until firm. Garnish with tomato slices. Makes 4 servings.

Note: Shrimp or crab meat can be substituted.

Fresh Tomato Aspic

    8 large tomatoes
    1 3-ounce package lemon-flavored gelatin
    2 tablespoons catsup
    1 tablespoon lemon juice
    1 tablespoon prepared horseradish
    1 teaspoon Worcestershire sauce
½ teaspoon salt
¾ cup diced celery
¼ cup diced onion
¼ cup diced green pepper

Scallop stem ends of tomatoes and remove slice from tops. Scoop out pulp and place in blender or processor; blend until pureed. Turn shells upside down to drain. Strain, measuring 2 cups pulp with juice. Combine pulp, juice and gelatin in a saucepan. Bring to a boil, stirring to dissolve gelatin. Stir in catsup, lemon juice, horseradish, Worcestershire sauce and salt. Chill until slightly thickened; fold in vegetables. Fill tomato shells with gelatin. Refrigerate until firm. Serve on spinach leaves and topped with a dollop of mayonnaise or sour cream, if desired. Makes 8 servings.

Cucumber Ring

    1 tablespoon unflavored gelatin
½ cup cold water
½ teaspoon salt
    4 cups creamed cottage cheese
    2 3-ounce packages cream cheese, softened
½ cup mayonnaise
    1 medium cucumber, pared, seeded and grated
    1 green onion, minced
⅔ cup finely chopped celery

Soften gelatin in cold water; add salt. Stir over low heat until gelatin is dissolved. Beat together cheeses. Add mayonnaise and gelatin. Stir in cucumber, onion and celery. Pour into a lightly oiled 6-cup ring mold. Chill 8 hours or overnight. Makes 6 servings.

Molded Salads

Red, White and Blue Mold

  1 3-ounce package strawberry gelatin
  1 pint strawberries, sliced
  2 envelopes unflavored gelatin
  ½ cup cold water
  4 tablespoons sugar
  2 cups sour cream
  1 3-ounce package lemon gelatin
  1 pint blueberries

Prepare strawberry gelatin as directed on package. Pour a ⅛-inch layer in the bottom of a lightly oiled 8-cup mold. Refrigerate 20 minutes or until firm. Arrange 6 to 8 strawberry slices on top of the gelatin layer. Pour a ¼-inch layer of gelatin over berries; refrigerate until almost firm. Refrigerate remaining strawberry gelatin until mixture mounds when dropped from a spoon. Fold in remaining strawberry slices; gently spoon into mold. Refrigerate until almost firm. Sprinkle unflavored gelatin over ½-cup water. Heat, stirring constantly, until dissolved. Add unflavored gelatin and 2 tablespoons of the sugar to the sour cream, mixing well. Pour over the molded strawberry layer; refrigerate until almost firm. Prepare lemon gelatin as directed on package. Combine ½-cup lemon gelatin and blueberries in the blender; blend at low speed until pureed. Add blueberry mixture to the remaining lemon gelatin; stir in remaining unflavored gelatin and remaining 2 tablespoons sugar. Refrigerate until mixture mounds when dropped from a spoon. Pour over sour cream layer; refrigerate until firm. Makes 12 servings.

Cherry Jubilee Mold

  1 16-ounce can pitted dark sweet cherries, drain, reserving liquid
  1 3-ounce package cherry gelatin
  ½ cup cream sherry
  1 3-ounce package cream cheese, cut in cubes
  1 16-ounce can pear halves, drained and chopped
  ¼ cup chopped pecans

Add enough water to cherry liquid to make 1½ cups. In a saucepan, combine liquid and gelatin. Heat, stirring constantly, until gelatin dissolves. Remove from heat and add sherry. Refrigerate until slightly thickened. Fold in cherries, cheese, pears and pecans. Pour into an oiled 4½-cup mold. Refrigerate until firm. Makes 8 servings.

Rice and Vegetable Ring

Cook rice the day ahead and chill overnight in Italian dressing.

  2 cups cooked rice
  ½ cup Italian Oil and Vinegar (Recipe on page 44)
  ½ cup mayonnaise
  1 cup sliced radishes
  1 cucumber, peeled, seeded and chopped
  2 small tomatoes, peeled, seeded and chopped
  1 green pepper, chopped
  ¼ cup chopped green onion
     Lettuce leaves
  1 pint cherry tomatoes

Combine rice and Italian dressing; cover and refrigerate several hours or overnight. Add mayonnaise to rice mixture and stir well. Fold in vegetables, except cherry tomatoes, and press tightly into an oiled 5½-cup ring mold. Cover and refrigerate 3 to 4 hours. Unmold on a lettuce-lined platter and fill center with cherry tomatoes. Makes 8 to 10 servings.

Cranberry Chicken Shari

Colorful!

  1 envelope unflavored gelatin
  ½ cup cold water
  1 1-pound can whole cranberry sauce
  1 9-ounce can crushed pineapple, drained
  ½ cup coarsely chopped walnuts
  1 tablespoon lemon juice

In a saucepan, soften gelatin in water. Place over low heat and stir until dissolved. Add cranberry sauce, pineapple, nuts and lemon juice; mix well. Pour in an 8-inch square baking dish and refrigerate until almost firm. Pour Chicken Layer over top and refrigerate until firm. Makes 8 servings.

Chicken Layer

  1 envelope unflavored gelatin
  ½ cup cold water
  1 cup mayonnaise
  3 tablespoons lemon juice
  ½ teaspoon salt
  ¼ teaspoon pepper
  2 cups cubed cooked chicken or turkey
  ½ cup diced celery
  2 tablespoons minced parsley

In a small saucepan, soften gelatin in water; place over low heat and stir until dissolved. Combine remaining ingredients. Add dissolved gelatin and mix well.

Molded Salads

Frozen Fruit Mold

- 1 envelope unflavored gelatin
- 1 cup cold water
- ⅓ cup sugar
- 2 tablespoons lemon juice
- 1 cup sour cream
- 2 3-ounce packages cream cheese, softened
- 1 11-ounce can mandarin oranges, drained
- 1 1-pound can sliced peaches, drained
- 1 30-ounce can pitted dark sweet cherries
- 2 cups miniature marshmallows
- 1 cup heavy cream, whipped
  Lettuce leaves

Sprinkle gelatin over cold water; place container over hot water, stirring to dissolve gelatin. In a mixing bowl, combine sugar, lemon juice, sour cream and cream cheese; beat until blended. Stir in gelatin mixture. Refrigerate until mixture is slightly thickened; beat until smooth. Fold in fruits, marshmallows and whipped cream. Pour into 2 refrigerator trays or 2 clean round No. 2 or No. 2½ fruit cans; freeze. Unmold and slice. Serve on lettuce leaves. Makes 8 to 10 servings.

Thirty-Minute Fruit Mold

- 1 envelope unflavored gelatin
- 2 tablespoons sugar
- ⅛ teaspoon salt
- ¾ cup water
- 1 6-ounce can any frozen juice concentrate, except pineapple
- 1 tablespoon lemon juice
- 3 ice cubes
- 1½ cups diced fruit, fresh or canned (do not use fresh pineapple)

In a saucepan, combine gelatin, sugar and salt. Add water and cook, stirring constantly, over low heat until gelatin dissolves. Remove from heat; add frozen juice concentrate, lemon juice and ice cubes. Stir until mixture is the consistency of unbeaten egg whites. Fold in fruit; pour into a lightly oiled 3-cup mold. Refrigerate 25 minutes or until firm. Makes 4 to 6 servings.

Bing Cherry Mold

- 2 3-ounce packages cherry or black cherry gelatin
- 2 cups boiling water
- 1 cup cold water
- 2 teaspoons lemon juice
- 2 tablespoons dry sherry
- 1 cup sour cream
- 2 cups pitted, halved, fresh Bing cherries
- ¼ cup toasted almonds (optional)

Dissolve gelatin in boiling water, stirring to dissolve; add cold water and lemon juice. To 1 cup of the gelatin mixture, add sherry; pour into an oiled 2-quart mold. Refrigerate until almost firm. Refrigerate remaining gelatin until slightly thickened; beat until fluffy. Fold in sour cream, cherries and almonds; pour over first layer and refrigerate 5 hours or overnight. Makes 10 to 12 servings.

Shrimp Mold

- 1½ tablespoons unflavored gelatin
- ¼ cup cold water
- 1 10-ounce can tomato soup
- 1 8-ounce package cream cheese, softened
- 9 ounces cooked shrimp, coarsley chopped
- 1 cup mayonnaise
- 1 small onion, grated
- ¾ cup diced celery
- 1 tablespoon prepared horseradish

Dissolve gelatin in cold water; set aside. In a medium-size saucepan, heat soup over low heat. Add gelatin mixture and stir until dissolved. Add cream cheese; remove from heat and beat until well blended. Add remaining ingredients. Pour into a well-oiled 1-quart mold. Chill until firm. Makes 8 to 10 servings.

Note: A 7-ounce can of tuna can be substituted for the shrimp.

Cranberry Mold

- 1 envelope unflavored gelatin
- 2 tablespoons sugar
- ¼ teaspoon salt
- 1 cup water
- ½ cup mayonnaise
- 2 tablespoons lemon juice
- 1 teaspoon grated lemon rind
- 1 1-pound can whole cranberry sauce
- 1 orange or apple, peeled and diced or 1 8½-ounce can pineapple tidbits, drained
- ¼ cup chopped walnuts

In a saucepan, combine gelatin, sugar and salt. Add water; cook, stirring constantly, over low heat until gelatin is dissolved. Remove from heat and stir in mayonnaise, lemon juice and lemon rind. Beat until foamy. Pour into an ice cube tray and freeze 10 to 15 minutes until firm around edges but soft in center. Beat until fluffy; fold in remaining ingredients. Pour into an oiled 4-cup mold and refrigerate until firm. Makes 6 servings.

Rhubarb Mold

    3 cups diced rhubarb
    2 cups sugar
    1 cup boiling water
    2 envelopes unflavored gelatin
    ½ cup cold water
    1 pint fresh strawberries
    1 cup heavy cream, whipped (optional)
    1 tablespoon sugar (optional)
    2 tablespoons Kirsch (optional)

In a saucepan, combine rhubarb, sugar and boiling water; cook until tender. Dissolve gelatin in cold water; add to rhubarb and stir until dissolved. Pour into an oiled 8-cup ring mold and refrigerate until firm. Unmold and fill center with fresh strawberries. Add sugar and Kirsch to whipped cream and serve with salad. Makes 10 to 12 servings.

Sour Cream Cucumber Mold

    2 3-ounce packages lime gelatin
    2 cups boiling water
    1 teaspoon salt
    ¼ cup vinegar
    2 tablespoons grated onion
    1 cup sour cream
    ½ cup mayonnaise
    2 cups cucumber, peeled, seeded and diced

Dissolve gelatin in boiling water. Stir in salt, vinegar and onion. Refrigerate until mixture begins to thicken. Beat until foamy. Blend sour cream with mayonnaise; add to gelatin and beat until smooth. Fold in cucumber and pour into an oiled 7-cup mold. Refrigerate until firm; unmold and garnish with greens. Makes 8 servings.

Low-Calorie Fruit Mold

    1 tablespoon unflavored gelatin
    2 tablespoons cold water
    ¼ cup boiling water
    1½ cups low-calorie ginger ale or lemon-lime soda
    1 tablespoon lemon juice
    2 cups fresh or drained canned fruit
      Cottage cheese
      Grated orange peel

Soften gelatin in cold water. Add boiling water and stir until dissolved; cool. Stir in ginger ale and lemon juice; refrigerate until slightly thickened. Fold in fruit and pour into a 4-cup mold or 4 individual molds. Refrigerate overnight. Serve with cottage cheese and garnish with grated orange peel. Makes 4 servings.

Orange-Pineapple Mold

    1 3-ounce package orange gelatin
    1 cup boiling water
    1 8½-ounce can crushed pineapple, undrained
    1 cup diced orange sections
    1 11-ounce can mandarin oranges, drained
    1 cup miniature marshmallows
    1 cup sour cream
    2 tablespoons mayonnaise
      Lettuce leaves

Dissolve gelatin in water. Add pineapple and refrigerate until slightly thickened. Fold in oranges and marshmallows. Pour into an 8 x 8 x 2-inch pan and refrigerate until firm. Combine sour cream and mayonnaise, mixing well. Spread over top of gelatin. Cut in squares and serve on lettuce leaves. Makes 6 to 8 servings.

Plum Mold

    1 30-ounce can pitted purple plums, drain, reserving liquid
      Burgundy wine
    1 tablespoon lemon juice
    3 envelopes unflavored gelatin
    1 cup cold water

Add wine to reserved plum liquid to make 3 cups less 1 tablespoon liquid. In a large bowl, pour plum liquid and lemon juice over plums; let stand for 1 hour. Soften gelatin in cold water. Measure 1 cup plum and wine liquid and heat to boiling. Add to gelatin and stir until dissolved; refrigerate until slightly thickened. Fold in plums and pour into a 1½-quart mold; refrigerate until firm. Makes 8 servings.

Pine-Cran Cheese Mold

    1 3-ounce package cherry gelatin
    1 cup boiling water
    1 tablespoon lemon juice
    1 3-ounce package cream cheese, softened
    ¼ cup mayonnaise
    ⅛ teaspoon salt
    1 1-pound can whole cranberry sauce
    1 8-ounce can crushed pineapple, drained
    ½ cup diced celery
    ¼ cup chopped pecans (optional)

Dissolve gelatin in boiling water. Add lemon juice, cheese, mayonnaise and salt and beat well. Refrigerate until mixture begins to thicken. Beat again until fluffy and smooth. Fold in cranberry sauce, pineapple, celery and pecans, if desired. Pour mixture into a lightly oiled 4-cup mold and refrigerate until firm. Makes 8 servings.

Orange-Grapefruit Ring

- 1 6-ounce package lemon gelatin
- 1½ cups boiling water
- 1 6-ounce can frozen orange juice concentrate, thawed
- 1 cup cold water
- 1 11-ounce can mandarin oranges, drain, reserving liquid
- 1 1-pound can grapefruit sections, drained, and chopped

Dissolve gelatin in boiling water. Add orange juice concentrate, cold water and mandarin orange liquid; refrigerate until slightly thickened. Fold in oranges and grapefruit. Pour into an oiled 6½-cup ring mold and refrigerate 5 hours or until firm. Makes 8 to 10 servings.

Strawberry-Orange Mold

- 2 3-ounce packages orange gelatin
- 2 cups boiling water
- 1½ cups cold water
- 2 teaspoons lemon juice
- 2 oranges, peeled and sectioned
- 14 strawberries
  Additional strawberries for garnish

Dissolve gelatin in boiling water. Add cold water and lemon juice; refrigerate until slightly thickened. Fold in oranges and strawberries. Pour mixture into an oiled 6-cup ring mold; refrigerate 4 to 5 hours or until firm. Unmold and garnish with strawberries. Makes 6 to 8 servings.

Lime and Lemon Cheese Mold

- 1 20-ounce can crushed pineapple, drain, reserving juice
- 1 3-ounce package lime gelatin
- 1 3-ounce package lemon gelatin
- 1½ cups boiling water
- 1 3-ounce package cream cheese
- 1 cup heavy cream, whipped

Add enough water to reserved juice to make 2 cups. Bring to a boil; remove from heat and add lime gelatin, stirring to dissolve. Refrigerate until mixture begins to thicken. Fold in pineapple; pour into an oiled 7-cup ring mold. Refrigerate until almost firm. Dissolve lemon gelatin in boiling water. Refrigerate until mixture begins to thicken. Blend in cream cheese and beat until light and fluffy. Fold in whipped cream; pour over lime layer. Refrigerate until firm. Unmold and garnish with greens and assorted fruits. Makes 8 servings.

Fish Mousse

- 2½ cups water
- 2 envelopes unflavored gelatin
- 1 small onion, sliced
- 2 teaspoons salt
- ½ teaspoon peppercorns
- ½ teaspoon basil
- 1 16-ounce package frozen flounder, pollock or cod fillets
- ½ cup mayonnaise
- 1 tablespoon lemon juice
- ¼ teaspoon Tabasco sauce
- ½ cup heavy cream, whipped
  Lemon wedges
  Ripe olives

In a large skillet, heat water; sprinkle gelatin over water and stir over low heat until gelatin is dissolved. Add onion, salt, peppercorns, and basil; bring to a boil. Reduce heat to low; cover and simmer 5 minutes. Add frozen fish; bring to a boil. Reduce heat to low; cover and simmer 15 minutes or until fish flakes easily with a fork. Remove fish from liquid; discard skin and bones. Strain liquid; if necessary, add water to make 2¼ cups liquid. Add fish to liquid and chill until mixture is thickened. In blender or processor blend fish, liquid, mayonnaise, lemon juice and Tabasco until smooth; fold in whipped cream. Pour mixture into an oiled fish mold or a 5-cup ring mold and refrigerate until firm, about 4 hours. Serve with lemon wedges and ripe olives. Makes 4 to 6 servings.

Salmon or Tuna Mousse

- 1 envelope unflavored gelatin
- 1½ cups chicken broth
- 1 tablespoon grated onion
- ½ teaspoon Tabasco sauce
- 1¼ cups salmon or tuna, drained and flaked
- ¼ cup chopped celery
- 2 tablespoons diced green pepper
- 1 cup heavy cream, whipped
- 1 cucumber, thinly sliced
  Watercress

In a saucepan, sprinkle gelatin over ½ cup of the chicken broth to soften. Place over low heat and stir until gelatin is dissolved. Remove from heat and stir in remaining broth, onion and Tabasco. Refrigerate mixture until slightly thickened. Fold in fish, celery and green pepper; fold in whipped cream. Pour into an oiled 4-cup mold and chill until firm. Garnish with thinly sliced cucumber and watercress. Makes 6 servings.

Salad Dressings

Mayonnaise

Nothing beats the homemade.

- 1 egg
- ¾ teaspoon salt
- ½ teaspoon dry mustard
- ¼ teaspoon paprika
- 1 tablespoon vinegar
- 1 tablespoon lemon juice
- 1 cup salad oil *or* ¾ cup salad oil and ¼ cup olive oil
- 1 tablespoon boiling water

In a food processor fitted with a plastic blade, or in a blender, combine egg, seasonings, vinegar, lemon juice and ¼ cup of the oil. Process until thoroughly blended. Slowly add remaining oil, drop by drop, blending until all oil is used. Blend in boiling water. Makes 1¼ cups.

Italian Oil and Vinegar

- ¾ cup olive oil
- ¼ cup red wine vinegar
- 2 teaspoons crushed dried oregano
- 2 teaspoons crushed dried basil
- 2 teaspoons grated onion
- 1 clove garlic, minced
- ¼ teaspoon salt
- ¼ teaspoon pepper

In a jar, combine all ingredients and shake well. Makes 1 cup.

Creamy Onion Dressing

- 1 envelope onion soup mix
- 2 cups sour cream
- ½ cup milk or buttermilk

In a small bowl, combine all ingredients; blend thoroughly. Add more milk, a teaspoon at a time, if a thinner dressing is desired. Chill before serving. Makes 2½ cups.

Lo-Cal Mayonnaise

- ½ cup cottage cheese
- 1 egg
- ⅛ teaspoon dry mustard
- ⅛ teaspoon freshly ground pepper
- 1 tablespoon tarragon vinegar

Combine all ingredients in a blender or food processor and process until smooth. Chill and serve over a green salad. Makes 1 cup.

Lo-Cal Tomato Dressing

- 1 8-ounce can tomato sauce
- 2 tablespoons vinegar
- 1 tablespoon Worcestershire sauce
- 1 teaspoon sugar
- 1 teaspoon grated onion
- 1 teaspoon prepared horseradish
- ½ teaspoon salt
- ⅛ teaspoon pepper
- Dash Tabasco sauce

In a jar, combine all ingredients and shake well. Makes 1 cup.

Blue Cheese and Wine Dressing

For tossed salad or sliced tomatoes.

- ¼ cup dry red wine
- 3 tablespoons red wine vinegar
- ¾ cup olive or salad oil
- 1 clove garlic, minced
- 1 teaspoon salt
- ½ teaspoon freshly ground pepper
- ½ teaspoon crushed basil leaves
- 2 ounces blue cheese, crumbled

Combine all ingredients except cheese in jar and shake vigorously. Chill 1 hour or more. Stir in cheese just before serving. Makes 1½ cups.

Louis Dressing

Excellent on seafood salads.

- ¾ cup mayonnaise
- ¼ cup chili sauce
- 2 tablespoons wine vinegar
- 2 tablespoons chopped parsley
- 1 teaspoon prepared horseradish
- ½ teaspoon Worcestershire sauce

Combine all ingredients in a small bowl; blend thoroughly. Refrigerate until ready to use. Makes 1 cup.

Oil and Vinegar

- ¾ cup vegetable oil
- ¼ cup red wine vinegar
- 3 teaspoons chopped chives
- 2 teaspoons chopped parsley
- 2 teaspoons thyme
- ¼ teaspoon salt
- ⅛ teaspoon pepper

In a jar, combine all ingredients and shake well. Use over a green or vegetable salad. Makes 1 cup.

Tarragon Dressing

- 6 tablespoons olive oil
- 3 tablespoons red wine vinegar
- 3 teaspoons tarragon leaves, crushed, *or*
  1 tablespoon fresh tarragon
- 1 clove garlic, minced
  Dash freshly ground pepper
  Dash cayenne pepper
- ¼ teaspoon salt

Combine all ingredients in a jar; shake to mix well. Serve with green salad. Makes ½ cup.

French Dressing I

A basic favorite.

- 1 cup wine vinegar
- 3 cups salad oil
  Salt and pepper to taste
- 1 teaspoon dry mustard
  Dash Tabasco sauce
  Dash Worcestershire sauce
- 1 teaspoon paprika
- ¼ cup tomato puree
- 1 teaspoon sugar

Combine all ingredients in a jar and shake, mixing thoroughly. Refrigerate. Makes 4 cups.

French Dressing II

- ¾ cup salad oil
- 3 tablespoons cider vinegar
- 1 teaspoon salt
- ½ teaspoon sugar
- ½ cup catsup
- 1 tablespoon Worcestershire sauce
- ¼ teaspoon paprika

Combine all ingredients in a jar; shake well to blend. Makes 1 cup.

Thousand Island Dressing

For green salad or sliced tomatoes.

- ¾ cup mayonnaise
- ½ cup chili sauce or catsup
- ¼ cup minced Spanish olives
- 1 hard-boiled egg, chopped
  Pepper to taste

Combine ingredients in a small bowl; mix well. Refrigerate until ready to use. Makes 1½ cups.

Mock Creme Fraiche

Classically served with fresh fruit.

- 1 cup sour cream
- 1 tablespoon firmly packed brown sugar
  Dash of salt
- ½ cup heavy cream, whipped

Combine sour cream, brown sugar and salt; mix well. Fold in whipped cream, 1 tablespoon at a time. Cover and chill 3 to 4 hours. Makes 1½ cups.

Sour Cream Dressing

- ½ cup sour cream or yogurt
- 1 tablespoon sugar
- 1 tablespoon vinegar
- ½ teaspoon salt
- ⅛ teaspoon pepper

In a small bowl, combine all ingredients; blend thoroughly. Chill before serving. Serve over green salad. Makes ½ cup.

Low-Calorie Herb Dressing

- 6 tablespoons water
- 1 tablespoon olive oil
- 2 tablespoons lemon juice
- ½ teaspoon garlic powder
- ¼ teaspoon oregano
- ¼ teaspoon dry mustard
- ¼ teaspoon salt
  Pepper to taste
- ¼ teaspoon tarragon
- ¼ teaspoon dill
- ¼ teaspoon sugar substitute (optional)

In a jar, combine all ingredients; shake well. Refrigerate until needed. Makes ¾ cup.

Oriental Dressing

- 1 cup yogurt
- ½ cup mayonnaise
- ¼ cup chopped water chestnuts
- ¼ cup chopped green pepper
- 2 teaspoons soy sauce
- ⅛ teaspoon ginger

In small bowl, combine all ingredients. Whisk to blend well. Cover and refrigerate. Makes 2 cups.

Sandwiches

It is said that the sandwich was invented by a nobleman and a gambler who, while on a winning streak, ordered his dinner roast placed between two slices of bread so that he could continue his game. The whole world was the winner. The sandwich is the most versatile way to eat: it can be breakfast, lunch, dinner, or a snack. It can be served hot or cold, dainty or hearty—the possibilities are endless. Our thanks to the Earl of Sandwich!

A two-week supply of sandwiches can be prepared at your convenience, wrapped tightly and stored in your freezer. Seal individual servings in self-sealing bags or bags sealed with a heating device. Use different breads for variety, spreading softened butter or margarine on each slice of fresh bread, then spreading the filling. When freezing sandwiches, use thin slices of meat or cheese, fish, poultry, peanut butter (mixed with ⅓ cup margarine) or cooked egg yolks. Cooked egg whites toughen when frozen, mayonnaise separates, lettuce greens and raw vegetables do not freeze well. Add lettuce or tomato, fresh and crisp from the refrigerator, when sandwiches are to be served. Fillings for sandwiches can be moistened with cream, milk, cream cheese, pickle relish, chili sauce, catsup, horseradish, or fruit juice.

Lunch box sandwiches will thaw 2 to 3 hours after removing them from the freezer. Party sandwiches can be arranged on serving trays while still frozen. Cover with plastic wrap and damp tea towels until thawed. Add garnishes just before serving.

Meat Sandwiches

Spud Burger

    1 pound ground beef
    1 cup shredded potatoes
    ¼ cup finely chopped onion
    1 teaspoon salt
    ¼ teaspoon pepper
    5 slices American or Cheddar cheese
    5 hamburger rolls, split
    5 red onion slices

Combine meat, potatoes, onions, salt and pepper; mix well and shape into 5 patties. Broil 4 to 5 minutes on each side, or to desired doneness. Top each patty with a cheese slice; broil just enough to melt cheese slightly. On bottom half of roll, layer onion slice, patty and top half of bun. Makes 5 servings.

Hot Pastrami with Tomato and Cheese

    12 slices rye bread, toasted on one side
    12 slices hot pastrami
    1 8-ounce can tomato paste
    1 medium sweet onion, thinly sliced
    6 slices Swiss cheese

On each of 6 slices of toasted bread, layer 2 slices pastrami, a dollop of tomato paste, a few onion rings and a slice of cheese. Broil until cheese melts and bubbles. Top with remaining toast. Serve with mustard. Makes 6 servings.

Blue Cheese Burger

    1 pound ground chuck
    ½ cup crumbled blue cheese
    1 teaspoon prepared mustard
    1 green onion, minced
    2 slices bacon, cut in half
    4 hamburger rolls, split and buttered

Shape meat into 8 thin patties. Combine cheese, onion and mustard; and place a quarter of mixture on the center of 4 of the patties. Top with remaining patties; press edges together to seal. Broil on one side for 5 to 6 minutes. Turn; place a slice of bacon on top of each and broil until bacon is crisp. Serve in hot, toasted rolls. Makes 4 servings.

Steak Sandwiches

    1½ pounds flank steak
    ½ cup Burgundy
    ¼ cup vegetable oil
    1 clove garlic, minced
    1 small onion, minced
    ¼ teaspoon pepper
    2 dozen Parker House rolls or 12 crusty rolls

Score both sides of steak ⅛-inch deep in a diamond pattern. Place in a shallow baking pan. Combine wine, oil, garlic, onion and pepper, mixing well; pour over steak. Marinate 3 to 4 hours or overnight. Broil 5 minutes on each side. Slice meat on the diagonal in wafer-thin slices. Serve in hot buttered rolls. Makes 8 to 10 servings.

Meat Sandwiches

Tenderloin Sandwich

Thin slices of tenderloin, garnished with various vegetables and served on toast, make a beautiful and elegant brunch or supper.

- ¼ pound butter
  Thin slices of tenderloin
  Large mushrooms, sliced
  Thinly sliced onion rings
  Green pepper, cut in strips
  Tomatoes, sliced
  Zucchini, sliced
  Worcestershire sauce
  Thin slices of hot buttered toast

Melt butter and sauté meat and a selection of any or all of the vegetables until meat is pink and vegetables are tender-crisp. Sprinkle with Worcestershire sauce; season with salt and pepper. Serve on toast.

Taco Burger

- 1 pound ground beef
- 1 cup crushed corn chips
- ¼ cup chili sauce
- 5 hamburger rolls, split
- 5 slices American or Cheddar cheese
  Tomato, chopped
  Avocado, chopped (optional)

Combine meat, chips and chili sauce; mix well and shape into 5 patties. Broil 4 to 5 minutes on each side, or to desired doneness. Top each patty with a slice of cheese; place under broiler long enough to melt slightly. Place tomatoes and avocado on bottom half of bun, top with patty and top half of bun. Makes 5 servings.

Tacos

Mexican zip; make trays of fixings and let each assemble his or her own.

- 1 pound ground beef, browned and drained
- 1 small can taco sauce
- 1 tablespoon chili powder
- 1 medium onion, chopped
- 2 tomatoes, chopped
- ½ head lettuce, shredded
- ½ pound Cheddar cheese, grated
- 12 taco shells

Combine beef, taco sauce and chili powder in a saucepan. Simmer 5 to 6 minutes. Fill taco shells with meat mixture. Serve with bowls of remaining ingredients. Makes 12 servings.

Stroganoff Burgers

- 1 pound ground chuck
- 1 tablespoon butter or margarine
- 1 small onion, minced
- 7 mushrooms, diced
- 1 teaspoon beef bouillon crystals
- ½ cup sour cream
- 1 teaspoon Worcestershire sauce
- 2 hamburger rolls, split and buttered *or* 2 French rolls, split and buttered
- 2 tablespoons minced parsley

Shape meat into 4 patties. In a frying pan, melt butter; sauté onion and mushrooms until tender. Add bouillon crystals, sour cream and Worcestershire sauce; heat to steaming. Broil patties 4 to 5 minutes on one side; turn and broil 2 to 3 minutes. Toast rolls. Top each roll half with a meat patty, a serving of sauce and a sprinkle of parsley. Makes 4 servings.

South Seas Burger

- 1 pound ground chuck
- 2 tablespoons soy sauce
- 1 8-ounce can crushed pineapple, drain, reserving juice
  Dash garlic powder
- 1 green pepper, chopped
- 1 small onion, minced
- 4 hamburger rolls, split and buttered

Shape beef into 4 patties. Combine soy sauce, pineapple juice and garlic powder. Baste patties with half of this marinade. Combine pineapple, pepper and onion. Broil patties for about 4 to 5 minutes on one side. Turn and top with a dollop of pineapple mixture and remaining marinade. Broil 2 to 3 minutes until sizzling. Toast rolls until golden on cut side; top with broiled patties and top slice of bun. Makes 4 servings.

Roast Pork

Roast pork and horseradish are great friends.

- 8 thin slices roast pork
- 8 slices buttered bread
- 4 lettuce leaves (optional)
- ¼ cup prepared mustard
- 2 tablespoons prepared horseradish

Place 2 slices of roast pork on each of 4 bread slices. Top with lettuce. Combine mustard and horseradish; mix well and spread on remaining bread slices. Place on top of pork and serve. Makes 4 servings.

Ham and Slaw

8 thin slices ham
4 thick slices tomato
1 cup slaw, well drained
8 slices buttered rye or pumpernickel bread

Place 2 slices ham, 1 slice tomato and ¼ cup slaw on each of 4 slices of bread. Top with remaining bread slices. Makes 4 servings.

Jonathan Hamwich

12 slices white bread
Mayonnaise
Mustard
12 slices baked ham
6 apples, thinly sliced
12 slices Swiss cheese

Spread bread with equal mayonnaise and mustard. Layer each bread slice with 1 slice ham, 4 slices apple and 1 slice Swiss cheese. Place on baking sheet and broil until cheese melts and is lightly browned. Serve hot. Makes 12 servings.

Swiss Grill

8 slices raisin bread
Butter
8 slices ham
8 slices Swiss cheese

Toast raisin bread on 1 side; butter other side. Place 1 slice ham and 1 slice cheese on buttered side of bread slices. Broil until cheese bubbles. Makes 8 servings.

Ham and Cheese Puff

Makes a supper when served with mugs of homemade soup.

8 slices pumpernickel, toasted on one side *or*
4 English muffins, split and toasted
8 thin slices ham
8 slices Swiss cheese
8 thin slices onion
8 thick slices tomato
Mayonnaise
Curry powder (optional)

Layer each slice of bread, or each muffin half, with 1 slice each of ham, cheese, onion, tomato; top with a dollop of mayonnaise. Sprinkle with curry powder, if desired. Broil until cheese bubbles. Makes 8 servings.

Ham and Cheese Hawaiian

A quick open-faced sandwich for brunch or lunch. For a crowd, prepare ahead of time and broil at the last minute.

8 thin slices of ham
4 slices pineapple
4 slices sharp Cheddar cheese
2 English muffins, split and toasted

Layer 2 slices ham, 1 pineapple slice and 1 cheese slice on each English muffin half. Broil until cheese is bubbly. Makes 4 servings.

Deviled Ham

3 cups ground ham
1 onion, minced
2 tablespoons sweet pickle relish
¼ cup margarine
¼ cup mayonnaise
¼ cup mustard
12 slices rye bread
6 tomato slices
Lettuce leaves

Combine first 6 ingredients, mixing well. Spread on bread slices. Top with sliced tomatoes and lettuce. Makes 6 servings.

Grilled Ham and Cheese

8 thin slices ham
8 thin slices mozzarella cheese
8 slices rye bread
Soft butter
Mustard

Layer 2 slices ham and 2 slices cheese on each of 4 bread slices. Spread 1 side of remaining 4 slices with mustard and place on top. Spread outsides of sandwiches with softened butter. In a hot frying pan, brown sandwiches; turn to brown the other side. Serve immediately. Makes 4 servings.

Broiled Cheese and Bacon

2 English muffins, split and buttered
4 thick slices tomato
4 thin slices onion
4 slices cheese
4 slices bacon, cut in half

Layer tomato, onion and cheese slices on top of each muffin half. Top each with 2 pieces of bacon. Broil until bacon is crisp and cheese is melted. Makes 4 servings.

Meat Sandwiches

Julienne Ham Salad Sandwich

- ½ cup mayonnaise
- ¼ teaspoon dry mustard
- 2 cups grated carrot
- 1 cup (¼-pound) julienne ham
- ½ cup raisins
- 8 slices dark bread

Stir mustard into mayonnaise. Add remaining ingredients except bread, mixing well. Divide filling among 4 bread slices. Top with remaining 4 slices bread. Makes 4 servings.

Note: Sandwiches may be made 24 hours in advance, wrapped and refrigerated.

Ham Loaf for Sandwiches

A bit of difference for ground ham.

- 5 cups ground cooked ham
- 1 medium onion, minced
- 1 egg, lightly beaten
- 1 piece bread soaked in ¼ cup milk
- ¼ cup catsup
- 2 tablespoons prepared mustard
- 1 tablespoon prepared horseradish

Combine all ingredients; mix well. Pour into a greased loaf pan and bake in a 350° oven 35 minutes. Cool and slice for sandwiches.

Ham Loaf Combinations

Ham Loaf with:
Cheese on rye bread.
Tomato and lettuce on a hard roll.
Sliced dill pickle on white bread.
Sliced hard-boiled egg with Thousand Island dressing.
Sliced turkey on pumpernickel bread.

Barbecued Pork

- 2 tablespoons margarine
- 1 onion, chopped
- 1 clove garlic, crushed
- 1 cup chili sauce
- 1 cup catsup
- ¼ cup wine vinegar
- 2 tablespoons brown sugar
- 2 tablespoons Worcestershire sauce
- 1 teaspoon dry mustard
- ½ teaspoon salt
- 3 cups shredded cooked pork
- 8 hamburger or hard rolls, split

In a frying pan, melt margarine; sauté onion and garlic until onion is tender. Add remaining ingredients except meat. Heat until bubbly; add meat and return to bubbly hot. Spoon into heated hamburger rolls and serve. Makes 6 to 8 servings.

Poor Boy

- 1 pound ground beef, browned and drained
- ⅓ cup grated Parmesan cheese
- ¼ cup minced onion
- 1 6-ounce can tomato paste
- 1 teaspoon salt
- ½ teaspoon pepper
- 1 loaf French bread, halved lengthwise
- 3 tomatoes, sliced
- 4 ounces mozzarella or Cheddar cheese, sliced

Combine beef, Parmesan, onion, tomato paste, salt, pepper; mix well. Pile on 2 halves of French bread. Bake in a preheated 350° oven 15 minutes. Arrange slices of tomato and cheese on top and broil 6 inches from heat about 10 minutes. Makes 4 servings.

Beef Burgundy Hero

Serve with broiled tomatoes and mixed green salad for dinner.

- 1 12-inch loaf Italian bread
  Butter
- 1 slice bacon, diced
- 1½ pounds tenderloin or flank steak, cut into julienne strips
- 1 tablespoon flour
- ¼ cup beef broth
- ½ cup Burgundy
- ⅛ teaspoon thyme
- 3 tablespoons tomato paste
- ½ bay leaf
- 1 tablespoon butter
- 12 small frozen onions
- 12 fresh mushrooms, sliced

Cut loaf in half lengthwise; hollow out each half. Butter insides; place under broiler to toast and set aside. Fry bacon; sauté steak in drippings. Sprinkle flour over meat in pan; stir. Add broth and Burgundy, stirring until thickened. Add thyme, tomato paste and bay leaf. Simmer gently. In another frying pan, melt butter; sauté onions and mushrooms until golden. Add onions and mushrooms to Burgundy mixture, mixing well. Spoon into bread boats. Warm in a 350° oven for 10 minutes, and serve hot. Makes 4 servings.

Meat Sandwiches

Reuben Hero

½ cup mayonnaise
¼ cup chili sauce
1 tablespoon grated onion
1 tablespoon lemon juice
2 cups shredded green cabbage
1 loaf unsliced dark rye bread
  Butter
4 tablespoons butter or margarine
6 slices cooked turkey
6 slices corned beef or baked ham
12 slices Swiss cheese

In a large bowl, combine mayonnaise, chili sauce, onion and lemon juice. Add cabbage and toss to mix well. Refrigerate for at least 1 hour. Drain cabbage. Slice bread lengthwise into 3 layers. Butter bottom layer of bread. Fold turkey slices in half and place on top. Spread one half of the cabbage over turkey. Fold 6 cheese slices in half and lay on top. Place middle slice of bread on top; spread with butter. Arrange corned beef slices, folded in half, on top; spread remaining cabbage over and top with 6 cheese slices folded in half. Top with crust. Slice and serve. Makes 4 to 6 servings.

Moussaka Hero

1 pound round steak, slightly frozen, thinly sliced in 3-inch strips
¼ cup vegetable oil
¾ teaspoon salt
⅛ teaspoon pepper
½ teaspoon garlic powder
2 cups cubed eggplant
½ cup chopped onion
1 3-ounce can sliced mushrooms, undrained
2 tomatoes, peeled and chopped
½ cup chili sauce
8 French rolls, split lengthwise
  Butter
4 slices (6 ounces) mozzarella cheese, cut in quarters
  Shredded lettuce

In a frying pan, heat oil and brown meat. Sprinkle with salt, pepper and garlic powder. Remove meat from pan and set aside. To drippings, add eggplant and onion; cook 5 minutes. Add meat, mushrooms and liquid, tomatoes, and chili sauce; cover. Simmer 25 to 30 minutes, stirring occasionally. Butter inside of rolls and toast under broiler until golden. Spoon mixture into rolls and top each with 2 pieces of cheese and a little lettuce. Makes 8 sandwiches.

Greek Hero

¼ cup butter or margarine
1½ pounds lamb, cubed
1 cup sliced onion
1 clove garlic, minced
3 tablespoons tomato paste
½ cup red wine
¼ cup chicken broth *or* 1 bouillon cube dissolved in ¼ cup water
1 teaspoon salt
⅛ teaspoon pepper
1 teaspoon oregano
¼ teaspoon thyme
¼ teaspoon rosemary
4 pitas, partially split
1 tomato, sliced
4 large onion slices
1 cup shredded lettuce

In a skillet, heat butter; brown lamb on all sides, a few pieces at a time. Remove lamb from pan as it browns. Add onion and garlic and sauté until golden. Return lamb to pan; add tomato paste, wine, broth and seasonings. Bring to a boil; reduce heat, cover and simmer 45 minutes, or until meat is tender. In a 350° oven, heat bread for 10 minutes; remove to platter. Fill each pocket of bread with the lamb mixture, tomato, onion and lettuce. Makes 4 servings.

Italian Sausage Hero

2 tablespoons salad or olive oil
1 green pepper, cut in ½-inch strips
1 medium yellow onion, sliced ¼ inch thick
1 4-ounce jar roasted sweet red peppers
4 sweet Italian sausages
4 hot Italian sausages
1 18 to 20-inch loaf Italian bread
6 tablespoons butter or margarine
6 slices Italian salami
  Lettuce leaves

Heat oil in skillet and sauté green pepper and onion about 10 minutes, or until tender-crisp. Stir in red peppers. Cook sausages about 20 minutes in skillet until browned and well done. Drain on paper toweling. Cut bread in half lengthwise and spread with butter. Warm in a 350° oven for 10 minutes. Remove from oven; on bottom half of loaf arrange sausages and salami. Top with pepper-onion mixture, lettuce leaves and top half of bread. Slice and serve. Makes 4 to 6 servings.

Hot Corned Beef-Turkey-Cheese Heroes

    8 hamburger buns or rye rolls, cut in half
      Mustard
    1 12-ounce can corned beef, chilled
    4 slices processed Swiss cheese, cut in half
      diagonally
    ½ pound thinly sliced turkey

Lightly spread cut surfaces of rolls with mustard. Cut chilled corned beef into 8 slices. Layer slices of corned beef, cheese and turkey on buns; replace top of buns. Wrap each roll in a square of aluminum foil and bake in a 350° oven for 20 minutes. Makes 8 servings.

Pizza Hero

    1 18 to 20-inch loaf Italian bread
    1½ pounds ground chuck
    1 small onion, minced
    1 clove garlic, minced
    1 8-ounce can tomato sauce
    ⅓ cup grated Romano cheese
    ½ teaspoon oregano
    1 8-ounce package mozzarella cheese, sliced
    2 green peppers, sliced
    2 large tomatoes, sliced
    1 2-ounce can anchovy fillets, drained

Slice bread lengthwise, then in half crosswise. In a frying pan, sauté meat, onion and garlic; drain fat. Add tomato sauce, Romano cheese and oregano; cook until heated through. Spoon meat mixture onto bread slices. Top with overlapping layers of mozzarella cheese, green pepper and tomatoes. Broil 6 inches from heat for 5 minutes, or until cheese is melted. Lay anchovy fillets on top and serve. Makes 4 servings.

Antipasto Hero

    1 12-inch loaf Italian bread
      Butter
    1 7-ounce can tuna, drained and flaked
    ½ pound cooked shrimp, chopped
    1 jar chili sauce
    ½ cup catsup
    1 teaspoon Worcestershire sauce
    1 4-ounce jar stuffed olives, sliced
    1 4-ounce can mushroom stems and pieces
    1 16-ounce jar sweet mixed pickles, diced
    1 cup mixed salad greens, torn into bite-size pieces

Slice loaf of bread in half, lengthwise; butter cut sides and toast. Set aside. Combine remaining ingredients. Refrigerate until chilled and heap onto bread. Makes 6 to 8 servings.

Chili Dogs

    4 hot dog rolls, split
    4 hot dogs, partially split lengthwise
      Chili
    1 small onion, chopped

Place hot dog in a roll. Spoon ¼ cup of the Chili over each hot dog. Broil 8 to 10 minutes, or until bubbly. Sprinkle with chopped onion and serve. Makes 4 servings.

Chili

    ½ pound ground chuck
    1 small onion, minced
    2 tablespoons tomato paste
    2 teaspoons chili powder
      Sprinkle garlic powder

Sauté beef and onion until done. Drain; stir in tomato paste, chili powder and garlic powder. Simmer until steaming.

Turkey Benedict

Something new for brunch or lunch.

    2 tablespoons butter
    2 tablespoons flour
    ½ teaspoon salt
    ⅛ teaspoon pepper
    1 cup milk
    1 cup grated Cheddar cheese
    ¼ teaspoon Worcestershire sauce
    6 slices ham or Canadian bacon
    6 slices cooked turkey
    6 English muffin halves, toasted

Melt butter in a saucepan over low heat. Add flour, salt and pepper, stirring until blended. Gradually stir in milk; cook, stirring constantly, until sauce is thickened and smooth. Lower heat and add grated cheese and Worcestershire sauce; stir until cheese is melted. Top each muffin half with a slice of ham or bacon and turkey. Pour hot cheese sauce over and serve. Makes 6 servings.

Cheese Dogs

    1 onion, diced
    ¼ cup catsup
    ½ pound Cheddar cheese, grated
    8 hot dog rolls, split
    8 hot dogs, partially split lengthwise

Combine onion, catsup and cheese; mix well. Place hot dogs in rolls and spoon onion mixture over. Broil 5 inches from heat for 8 to 10 minutes, or until cheese melts and hot dogs sizzle. Makes 8 servings.

Meat Sandwiches

Greek Pitas

Garnish with ripe olives and cherry tomatoes.

- 8 thin slices roast lamb
- 4 thick slices large tomato
- 4 thin slices sweet onion
- 4 Pitas *or* 8 slices dark rye bread, buttered
- ½ cucumber, thinly sliced
- ½ cup sour cream

Layer lamb, tomato, onion and cucumbers in pockets of Pitas or on 4 slices of bread. Top with a dollop of sour cream. Makes 4 servings.

Liverwurst and Onion Sandwich

Hearty fare for big appetites.

- ½ pound bacon, cooked crisp and drained
- 1 large onion, sliced in rings
- 12 slices liverwurst
- 4 English muffins, sliced, buttered, toasted

Sauté onion rings in bacon drippings; drain. Place 3 liverwurst slices on each of 4 muffin halves. Top with onion rings, bacon slices and tops of muffins. Makes 4 servings.

Mock Paté

- ½ pound liverwurst, mashed
- 1 3-ounce package cream cheese
- 6 black olives, sliced
- ¼ cup chopped chives
- ⅛ cup butter or margarine
- 1 teaspoon prepared mustard
  Lettuce leaves
- 8 slices rye or pumpernickel bread, buttered

Combine first 6 ingredients; mix well. Divide among 4 bread slices. Top each with a lettuce leaf and second slice of bread. Makes 4 servings.

Chicken Livers en Brochette Sandwich

- 1 pound chicken livers
- 4 slices bacon, cut into 1-inch squares
- 12 cherry tomatoes
- 2 small onions, quartered
- 1 green pepper, cut into large chunks
- ½ cup chili sauce
- 2 tablespoons Worcestershire sauce
- 4 French rolls, split and buttered

Thread livers, bacon, tomatoes, onions and peppers onto 4 skewers. Combine chili sauce and Worcestershire sauce; brush onto liver brochettes. Broil until bacon and livers are crispy and done. Place a skewer in each roll; remove skewer. Makes 4 servings.

Thousand Island Sandwich

Garnish with tomato wedges and black olives for a picture-pretty luncheon.

- 4 slices rye bread, buttered
- 4 slices ham or corned beef
- 4 slices roast turkey
- ½ head lettuce, shredded
- 1 cup Thousand Island Dressing

On each slice of bread, place a slice of ham and a slice of turkey. Top with shredded lettuce and drizzle Thousand Island dressing lightly over all. Serve with remaining dressing. Makes 4 servings.

Thousand Island Dressing

- ¾ cup mayonnaise
- ¼ cup chili sauce
- 1 teaspoon Worcestershire sauce
- 1 green onion, minced (optional)

In a small mixing bowl, combine all ingredients. Beat with a whisk to blend.

Chicken Pita

- 1 avocado, diced
- 1 tablespoon lemon juice
- 2½ cups diced cooked chicken
- 1 small onion, minced
- 2 roasted red chilies, seeded, chopped (optional)
- ½ cup mayonnaise
- 4 pita breads

Toss diced avocado in lemon juice. Add remaining ingredients, except pitas, and toss lightly. Heat pitas in a 350° oven; fill with chicken mixture. Makes 4 servings.

Monte Cristo au Gratin

- 6 slices bread
- 12 slices of turkey or ham or 6 slices each
- 3 eggs, lightly beaten with 2 tablespoons water
- 2 tablespoons vegetable oil
- 1 tablespoon butter
- 1½ cups grated processed Swiss cheese
- ½ cup milk
- ½ cup mayonnaise
- ⅛ teaspoon nutmeg

Place meat between 2 slices of bread. Dip sandwiches in egg mixture. In a frying pan, heat oil and butter; fry both sides of sandwiches until golden brown. Place in a baking dish. In a saucepan, combine cheese, milk, mayonnaise and nutmeg. Heat, stirring constantly, until cheese melts and mixture is smooth. Pour over sandwiches and broil 3 to 5 minutes, 6 inches from broiler, until bubbly. Makes 3 servings.

Meat Sandwiches

Turkey au Gratin

    3 tablespoons butter
    3 tablespoons flour
1½ cups milk
    ¼ cup dry sherry
    ¼ teaspoon salt
    ⅛ teaspoon pepper
    2 tablespoons butter
    ¼ pound mushrooms, sliced
    3 slices toast cut in half diagonally
12 slices turkey
    ½ cup grated Parmesan cheese

In a frying pan, melt the 3 tablespoons butter. Add flour, stirring until golden. In a saucepan, heat milk; gradually add to flour mixture, stirring until thickened. Add sherry, salt and pepper. In another frying pan, melt the 2 tablespoons butter; sauté mushrooms 5 minutes. Add to sauce. Arrange toast halves in a flat casserole; divide turkey slices among toast. Pour sauce over all and sprinkle with Parmesan cheese. Broil until bubbly and golden. Makes 3 to 6 servings.

Chicken Salad Sandwich

    2 cups finely chopped cooked chicken
    ½ cup minced celery
    ½ cup minced ripe olives (optional)
    ¾ cup mayonnaise
    1 teaspoon vinegar
12 slices buttered bread
    6 lettuce leaves

Combine first 5 ingredients; mix well. Place a lettuce leaf on each of 6 slices of bread. Spoon on chicken salad and top with remaining bread slices. Makes 6 servings.

Grilled Turkey and Cheese

Serve with tomato wedges and cucumber slices.

    ½ cup mayonnaise
    2 tablespoons prepared mustard
    1 tablespoon horseradish (optional)
11 ripe olives, sliced
    8 slices bread
    8 thin slices roast turkey
    8 slices Monterey Jack cheese

Combine mayonnaise, mustard, horseradish and olives; mix well. Toast one side of bread; butter other side. Place a slice of turkey on buttered side of bread. Top each with a slice of cheese and 1 to 2 tablespoons of the mayonnaise mixture. Broil until cheese bubbles. Makes 8 servings.

Turkey Loaf

A new way to enjoy turkey.

    5 cups minced cooked turkey
    1 cup cooked stuffing *or* ¾ cup seasoned
      bread crumbs
    1 small onion, minced
    1 rib celery, chopped
    ½ green pepper, chopped
    1 egg, lightly beaten
    ¼ cup chopped parsley

Combine all ingredients; mix well. Pour into a greased loaf pan; bake in a 350° oven 35 minutes. Cool and slice for sandwiches.

Turkey Loaf Combinations

Turkey loaf with:
    Cranberry sauce on white bread.
    Leftover hot gravy over toast.
    Swiss cheese.
    Lettuce and mayonnaise.
    Sliced ham.

Sausage and Rye

Serve with big, crunchy dill pickles and pass the hot mustard.

    8 large slices rye bread, toasted on one side
      Butter
    1 6-ounce can tomato paste
    8 Polish sausages, cut in half lengthwise
    8 slices Swiss cheese

Butter untoasted side of bread; spread 1 tablespoon tomato paste on each slice. Place 2 halves of Polish sausage on each slice; broil until sausage sizzles. Top each with a cheese slice; broil until cheese melts. Makes 8 servings.

Corned Beef and Cheese

    ¼ cup shredded sharp Cheddar cheese
    2 tablespoons mayonnaise
    4 ounces corned beef, shredded
    ¼ cup finely chopped dill pickles
    1 tablespoon grated onion
      Salt and pepper to taste
      Worcestershire sauce to taste
12 slices rye bread

Cream together cheese and mayonnaise. Add remaining ingredients, except bread, and mix well. Spread on bread slices. May be garnished with lettuce and tomato slices. Makes 6 servings.

Tuna Turnovers

    1 7-ounce can tuna, drained and flaked
    4 ounces Monterey Jack cheese, cubed
    ¼ cup mayonnaise
    1 teaspoon tomato paste
    ½ cup bean sprouts
    1 8-ounce package refrigerated biscuits
    1 egg, lightly beaten

Combine first 5 ingredients; mix well. Separate biscuits. On a lightly floured board, roll out each biscuit into a 5-inch circle. Place a spoonful of tuna mixture on 5 biscuits and top each with a biscuit. Seal edges with a fork dipped in flour. Repeat process, making 5 turnovers. Place on a greased cookie sheet; brush with egg. Bake in a 350° oven 15 minutes, or until lightly browned. Remove at once. Set aside 10 minutes. Serve warm or cold. Makes 5 servings.

Tuna Rolls

    ¼ pound American or Cheddar cheese, cubed
    3 hard-boiled eggs, finely chopped
    1 7-ounce can tuna, drained
    2 tablespoons diced green pepper
    1 tablespoon sliced green olives
    1 tablespoon chopped onion
    ½ cup mayonnaise
    ¾ teaspoon salt
    6 hot dog rolls, split

Combine all ingredients except hot dog rolls; mix well. Divide among rolls. Broil until cheese melts. Makes 6 servings.

Mock Lobster Salad Sandwich

    ½ cup chicken broth
    ½ cup dry white wine
    1 tablespoon lemon juice
    1 pound cod fillets
    1 rib celery, chopped
    ¾ cup mayonnaise
    1 tablespoon lemon juice
    1 teaspoon prepared horseradish
    1 green onion, minced, white only
       Few drops Tabasco
   18 small rolls or 12 thin slices white toast

In a large frying pan, combine broth, wine and lemon juice. Add cod and simmer 6 to 8 minutes, or until fish is white and flakes easily with a fork. Drain and refrigerate until cold. Flake cod into small pieces. Add remaining ingredients except rolls, mixing well; refrigerate to chill. Spread between rolls or on 6 slices toast; top with remaining toast slices. Makes 6 or 18 servings.

Tuna Melts

    1 7-ounce can tuna, drained and rinsed
    ¼ cup mayonnaise
    2 tablespoons chili sauce
   12 green stuffed olives, sliced (optional)
    1 rib celery, diced
    ½ teaspoon Worcestershire sauce
    ½ cup grated American cheese
    6 slices bread, toasted on 1 side

Combine all ingredients except cheese and bread; mix well. Spread on untoasted sides of bread slices. Sprinkle with cheese and broil about 5 minutes, or until cheese melts. Makes 6 servings.

Salmon Loaf

    1 1-pound can salmon, drained, bones, skin and
       fat removed
    ½ cup cracker crumbs
    1 small onion, minced
    ½ rib celery, diced
    1 egg, lightly beaten
    1 teaspoon prepared mustard
    1 teaspoon Worcestershire sauce
    1 teaspoon lemon juice
    1 tablespoon sherry
    ¼ cup sour cream

Combine all ingredients; mix well. Pour into a greased loaf pan and bake in a 350° oven 35 minutes. Cool and slice for sandwiches.

Salmon Loaf Combinations

Salmon loaf with:
    Cucumber and chives on rye.
    Cream cheese and chopped celery and green
       pepper.
    Lettuce and mayonnaise.
    Sliced black olives.

Salmon Salad

    1 6-ounce can red salmon, drained, flaked, bones
       and skin discarded
    1 rib celery, chopped
    1 small onion, minced
    1 tablespoon lemon juice
    ¼ teaspoon black pepper
    2 tablespoons mayonnaise
    1 tablespoon sour half and half
       Lettuce leaves
    8 thin slices bread, buttered

Combine first 7 ingredients; mix well. Spread on 4 bread slices. Top each with a lettuce leaf and the remaining bread slices. Makes 4 servings.

Crabcake Sandwich

    1 pound crabmeat, cartilage removed
    ½ cup cracker crumbs
    1 egg, lightly beaten
    2 teaspoons prepared mustard
    ¼ cup minced parsley
    ¼ cup butter
    6 soft rolls

Combine first 5 ingredients; mix gently. Form into 6 patties. In a frying pan, melt butter; sauté patties until golden brown. Serve immediately on rolls. Makes 6 servings.

Not-for-Sissies Sardines

    1 3-ounce package cream cheese
    3 ounces blue cheese, crumbled
    ½ small onion, minced
    1 tablespoon lemon juice
    8 thin slices white bread, buttered
    1 can sardine fillets, drained
      Lettuce leaves

Combine cheeses, onion and lemon juice; mix well. Divide mixture among 4 slices bread. Top each with sardine fillets, lettuce leaf and second slice of bread. Makes 4 servings.

Quick Fish Sandwich

    6 frozen, breaded fish fillets
    6 sesame rolls, split and buttered
    ½ cup mayonnaise
    2 tablespoons pickle relish (sweet or dill)
    1 teaspoon prepared mustard
    ½ small onion, minced

Prepare fish according to package directions. Butter rolls and toast. Prepare sandwiches. Combine remaining ingredients; mix well. Serve with fish sandwiches. Makes 6 servings.

California Crab Salad Sandwich

    1 avocado, peeled and cut into thin wedges
    ¼ cup lemon juice
    6 ounces crab meat, flaked
    ½ small rib celery, diced
    ½ cup mayonnaise
    6 lettuce leaves
    6 thin pieces whole wheat toast
    6 slices avocado
    ½ cup alfalfa sprouts

Brush avocado with part of the lemon juice. Combine crab meat, celery, mayonnaise and remaining lemon juice; mix well. Place a lettuce leaf on each piece of toast. Top with crab salad and an avocado slice. Garnish with a generous sprinkling of alfalfa sprouts. Makes 6 servings.

Shrimp Sandwiches

    2 8-ounce packages cream cheese, softened
    ½ cup chili sauce
    2 tablespoons prepared horseradish
    1 teaspoon Tabasco sauce
    1 teaspoon lemon juice
    1 teaspoon Worcestershire sauce
    ½ pound shrimp, cut up
    ½ cup diced celery
    6 slices white bread, toasted

Combine all ingredients, except bread; mix well. Spread shrimp mixture on toast. Serve open faced; if desired, garnish each with a cucumber slice. Makes 6 servings.

Tuna Salad

    1 7-ounce can water-packed tuna, drained
      and flaked
    6 water chestnuts, sliced
    1 rib celery, minced
    ½ green pepper, chopped
    1 large sweet pickle, chopped or 1 tablespoon
      sweet pickle relish
    ¼ cup mayonnaise
    ¼ cup sour half and half
    2 teaspoons curry powder
    8 slices toast
      Lettuce leaves

Combine first 8 ingredients; mix well. Divide tuna mixture among 4 toast slices. Top each with a lettuce leaf and remaining toast slices. Makes 4 servings.

Caviar Sandwich

Special occasions deserve special attention. Serve with scrambled eggs and champagne for a midnight supper or late brunch.

    1 8-ounce package cream cheese, softened
    3 green onions, minced
    3 tablespoons mayonnaise
    8 slices thin white bread, toasted
    1 3-ounce jar caviar (red or black)
      Lemon wedges

Combine cream cheese, onion and mayonnaise; mix well. Divide among bread slices. Sprinkle caviar onto each piece; garnish with lemon wedge. Makes 8 servings.

Egg and Cheese Sandwiches

Apple-Cheese Sandwich Spread

    1 cup coarsely chopped apple
    1 cup grated sharp Cheddar cheese
    ½ cup raisins
    ½ cup chopped walnuts
    2 tablespoons lemon juice
    ½ cup mayonnaise
   12 thin slices rye bread

Combine apple, cheese, raisins, walnuts and lemon juice; mix with enough mayonnaise to hold the ingredients together. Spread on 6 bread slices; top with remaining slices. Makes 6 servings.

Deviled Egg Sandwich

    8 hard-boiled eggs, chopped
    ½ cup mayonnaise
    1 teaspoon vinegar
    1 tablespoon mustard
    1 tablespoon Worcestershire sauce
    1 tablespoon minced sweet pickle
   16 slices whole wheat bread, buttered
      Lettuce leaves

Combine all ingredients except bread and lettuce; mix well. Spread on 8 slices bread. Top with a lettuce leaf and remaining bread slices. Makes 8 servings.

Corned Beef Hash Surprise

    6 English muffins, split and toasted
    1 can corned beef hash, cut into 6 slices
    6 poached eggs
      Chili sauce (optional)

Place 1 slice of corned beef hash on each of 6 muffin halves. Broil until crispy brown. Top with a poached egg and the remaining muffin half. Serve with chili sauce, if desired. Makes 6 servings.

Cream Cheese and Marmalade

Delicious combination of mild and bittersweet; very tasty on toasted English muffins or raisin bread.

    1 3-ounce package cream cheese, softened
    2 tablespoons butter or margarine, softened
    2 tablespoons bitter orange marmalade
    2 English muffins, split and toasted *or* 4 slices
      raisin toast

Combine cream cheese, butter, and marmalade; beat until smooth. Spread on hot muffin halves or toast. Makes 4 servings.

Egg and Anchovy Sandwich

Eggs and anchovies go well together.

    6 hard-boiled eggs, minced
    ¼ cup mayonnaise
    1 tablespoon lemon juice
    1 can anchovies and capers, drained and minced
      Pepper to taste
   12 slices thin white bread or toast

Combine the first 5 ingredients; mix well. Heap onto 6 slices of bread. Top with remaining slices. Makes 6 servings.

Egg Salad with Chives

Chives make the difference.

    4 hard-boiled eggs, chopped
    ¼ cup chopped celery
    ¼ cup chopped green pepper
    ¼ cup minced chives
    3 tablespoons sour cream
    3 tablespoons mayonnaise
    ½ teaspoon salt
    ¼ white pepper
    ½ teaspoon curry powder (optional)
    4 slices bread, buttered and toasted

Combine all ingredients except toasted bread; mix well. Spread on 2 slices hot, toasted bread and top with remaining slices. Makes 2 servings.

Blue Cheese Spread

    1 8-ounce package cream cheese, softened
    1 4-ounce package blue cheese, softened
    3 green onions, chopped
    ¼ cup mayonnaise
    1 tablespoon mustard
   12 slices thin bread

Combine all ingredients except bread. Mix well and spread on 6 slices bread. Top with remaining bread slices. Makes 6 servings.

Pimiento-Cheese Spread

   10 ounces sharp Cheddar cheese, grated
    1 8-ounce package cream cheese, softened
    ½ onion, minced
    ½ cup chili sauce
    ¼ cup minced pimiento (or to taste)
    ¼ cup sour half and half
   16 slices white bread

Combine all ingredients except bread; mix well. Spread on 8 slices bread. Top with remaining slices. Serve cold or butter outside of sandwiches and broil until cheese melts. Makes 8 servings.

Deviled Cheddar

- 10 ounces sharp Cheddar cheese, grated
- 1 8-ounce package cream cheese, softened
- ½ onion, minced
- ¼ cup chili sauce
- 1 tablespoon Worcestershire sauce
- 1 tablespoon prepared mustard
- ¼ cup margarine *or* ¼ cup mayonnaise
- 24 slices rye or pumpernickel bread

Combine all ingredients except bread; mix well. Divide among 12 slices bread; top with remaining 12 slices. Makes 12 servings.

Cheese and Tomato Sandwich

- 2 cups grated sharp Cheddar cheese
- 1 tablespoon mayonnaise
- 2 green onions, minced
- 1 teaspoon prepared mustard
- 1 teaspoon Worcestershire sauce
- 4 English muffins, split and toasted
- 8 slices tomato
    Butter

Combine first 5 ingredients; mix well. Divide mixture among 8 muffin halves. Broil for 2 to 3 minutes or until cheese starts to melt. Top each muffin with a tomato slice and a dot of butter. Return to broiler until butter bubbles. Makes 8 servings.

Watercress Triangles

- 1 8-ounce package cream cheese, softened
- ¼ cup margarine
- 2 tablespoons mayonnaise
- 3 green onions, minced
- 2 bunches watercress, chopped
- 12 thin slices white bread, crusts removed

Combine all ingredients except bread; mix well. Spread mixture on 6 bread slices; top with remaining slices. Cut each sandwich into quarters. To serve, stand sandwiches on end. Makes 6 servings.

Olive-Nut Sandwich

- 1 8-ounce package cream cheese, softened
- 12 pimiento stuffed or black olives, chopped
- ½ cup chopped walnuts
- ¼ cup mayonnaise
- 16 slices thin white bread

Combine cheese, olives, nuts and mayonnaise; mix well. Divide among 8 slices of bread. Top each with remaining bread slices. Makes 8 servings.

Mushroom Sandwich

- 2 tablespoons butter
- ¼ pound mushrooms, minced
- 1 clove garlic, minced
- 1 teaspoon sherry
- 1 3-ounce package cream cheese, softened
- 12 Parker House rolls, split

In a frying pan, heat butter until foamy; sauté mushrooms and garlic until golden. Add sherry. Pour mixture into cream cheese; blend thoroughly. Spoon into rolls and heat in a 325° oven 6 to 8 minutes. Serve with chicken salad, cold roast beef or pork. Makes 12 servings.

Asparagus Sandwiches

- 1 3-ounce package cream cheese, softened
- 1 small onion, minced
- 1 tablespoon mayonnaise
- 1 tablespoon capers
- 4 slices bread, buttered and toasted
- 1 can asparagus spears, drained
- 1 hard-boiled egg, minced
- 2 tablespoons oil and vinegar dressing (optional)

Combine cream cheese, onion, mayonnaise and capers; mix well. Spread on toast. Arrange asparagus spears on top and garnish with egg. Drizzle a little dressing over each, if desired. Serve at once. Makes 4 servings.

Tea Sandwich

- 1 pound cake
- 1 3-ounce package cream cheese, softened
- 1 tablespoon confectioners' sugar
- 1 tablespoon frozen orange juice concentrate, thawed
- 1 teaspoon grated lemon rind

Slice pound cake vertically into thin slices. Combine cream cheese, sugar, orange juice and lemon rind; beat to mix well. Spread on half the slices of pound cake. Top each with remaining slices; cut each slice into triangles or quarter for "fingers." Makes 18 to 24 servings.

Ambrosia Sandwich

- 1 loaf lemon tea bread, thinly sliced
- ½ cup butter, softened
    Apricot jam
- ¼ cup toasted coconut

Spread each bread slice with butter, then jam and a sprinkle of toasted coconut. Cut into "fingers" or triangles. Makes 18 to 24 servings.

Frosted Sandwich Loaf

1 day-old unsliced sandwich loaf, trimmed on all
  sides and sliced lengthwise into 4 equal slices

Egg Salad Filling

4 hard-boiled eggs, chopped
3 tablespoons mayonnaise
2 teaspoons prepared mustard
1 teaspoon grated onion
½ teaspoon salt

Ham or Tuna Filling

1 cup ground cooked ham or flaked tuna
⅓ cup mayonnaise
2 tablespoons pickle relish

Chicken Filling

1 cup minced chicken
¼ cup finely chopped celery
¼ cup mayonnaise

Frosting

11 ounces cream cheese, softened
5 tablespoons milk

In individual bowls, prepare each filling by combining ingredients and mixing well. Spread bread slices with softened butter or margarine. Spread first buttered slice with Egg Salad Filling; top with second slice and spread with Ham Filling; top with third slice and spread with Chicken Filling. Top with fourth slice. Combine cream cheese and milk; beat until fluffy. Smoothly spread top and sides of loaf with frosting. Decorate as desired. To serve, slice through all 4 layers. Makes 10 servings.

Spinach Sandwich

1 cup cottage cheese
3 green onions, cut in pieces
1 package frozen, chopped spinach, cooked and
  squeezed dry
4 water chestnuts, diced
2 tablespoons mayonnaise
1 teaspoon horseradish
6 wafer-thin slices ham
12 slices rye bread, buttered

In a blender, combine cottage cheese, onion and spinach; blend until smooth. Stir in water chestnuts, mayonnaise and horseradish. Place a slice of ham and 2 tablespoons spinach mixture on each of 6 slices of bread; top with remaining bread slices. Makes 6 servings.

Gazpacho Sandwich

½ cucumber, peeled, thinly sliced
2 tomatoes, chopped
1 small onion, chopped
1 green pepper, chopped
1 rib celery, chopped
2 tablespoons minced pimiento
1 tablespoon sweet pickle relish
1 teaspoon capers (optional)
2 tablespoons olive oil
1 tablespoon red wine vinegar
  Salt and pepper to taste
6 hard rolls
  Butter

Combine all ingredients except rolls and butter; mix well. Refrigerate 3 to 4 hours. Scoop out interior of hard rolls; butter inside and heat. Drain filling and heap into rolls. Makes 6 servings.

Ginger Tea Sandwiches

1 8-ounce package cream cheese, softened
1 tablespoon confectioners' sugar
1 teaspoon milk, if necessary
1 loaf pumpkin or nut bread, thinly sliced
  Candied ginger, cut into thin slivers

Combine cream cheese and sugar; beat until smooth, adding milk if needed to thin. Spread on each bread slice; top with slivers of ginger to taste. Cut into triangles and serve. Makes 18 to 24 servings.

Borscht Sandwich

1 1-pound can beets, minced and drained
1 small onion, minced
2 tablespoons horseradish
¼ cup sour cream
8 slices dark pumpernickel, buttered

Press beets to remove juice. Add remaining ingredients; mix well. Heap filling onto 4 buttered bread slices. Top with remaining slices. Makes 4 servings.

Radish Sandwich

¼ cup butter or margarine, softened
20 large radishes, thinly sliced
1 loaf party pumpernickel bread
  Chopped parsley for garnish

Spread bread slices with a rather heavy layer of butter. Overlap radish slices on top. Sprinkle a little parsley on each. Makes 18 to 20 servings.

Index

E
F
G
H
I
K
L
M